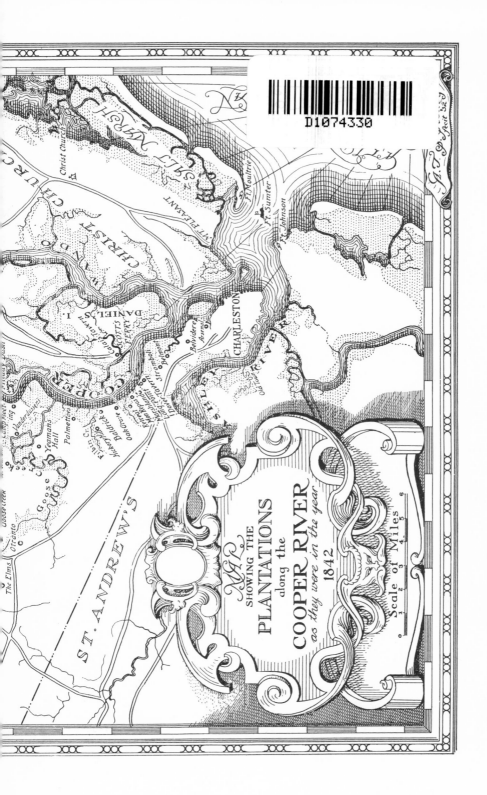

MAP
SHOWING THE
PLANTATIONS
along the
COOPER RIVER
as they were in the year
1842

Scale of Miles

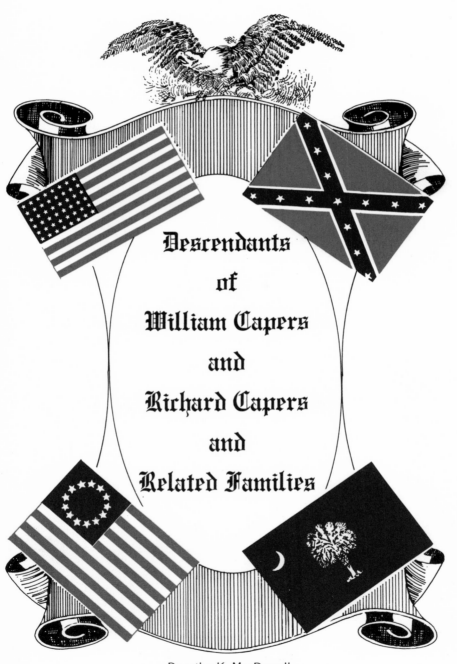

Descendants
of
William Capers
and
Richard Capers
and
Related Families

Dorothy K. MacDowell
(Mrs. McNeely DuBose MacDowell)

Printed by

THE R. L. BRYAN COMPANY
COLUMBIA, S. C.

ACKNOWLEDGEMENTS

There were many who gave information and assistance in this project, for which I am most grateful. I would especially like to thank Mrs. James B. Baggott of North Augusta, S. C.; Mrs. Edmund A. Burns of Charleston, S. C.; Mrs. Henry DeS. Bull of Georgetown, S. C.; Frank W. Capers IV, Esq. of Augusta, Ga.; Mrs. Louis W. Erath of Houston, Texas; the Rev. Silas Emmett Lucas, Editor of the *Georgia Genealogical Quarterly,* Easley, S. C.; Mrs. Donald S. Marmaduke of Denver, Col.; Mrs. Marvin A. Owings of Clemson, S. C.; Miss Emmalise P. Stone, of Oxford, Ga.; Mr. Charles E. Thomas of Greenville, S. C.; and Mr. W. H. J. Thomas of Charleston, S. C.

My thanks also to Mr. W. Legare McIntosh and his staff at The R. L. Bryan Co. for their interest and cooperation.

And last, *but foremost,* my deepest appreciation to William Manigault Capers, Esq. of Columbia, S. C. for his assistance, patience, faith, friendship, and financial aid. Without him this book would not have been.

DOROTHY K. MACDOWELL

113 Gregg Ave.
Aiken, S. C. 29801
July 1973

Diocese of South Carolina.

Bishop's Residence, Columbia, 4-7-'99.

My Dear Cousin: I am just home from visitations in the lower part of the Diocese, and find your letter of the 30th ultimo to Mrs. Capers.

I have read your sketch and looked at the crest and coat of arms with much interest. I have been so much away from home and so little time at my command when I am here, I have not been able to add anything to what you have written.

After carefully reading the matter sent us, I am satisfied that you have secured a trustworthy Coat of Arms.

Mrs. Capers unites with me in loving regards to you and your family.

Faithfully your cousin,

ELLISON CAPERS.

Mr. F. L. Capers, Pueblo, Colo.

My Dear Mr. Capers: I have, after many months, found in the possession of Miss Marion Thayer Capers, of Crystal Springs, Miss., the seal of her great, great grandfather Capers. This seal bears the authentic Arms of the Capers family. A description of the Arms is as follows:

Three foxes passant argent in pale, over all a crescent argent. Crest, a bunch of grapes proper.

The original name was Capier, and undoubtedly they were Hugenots. They went from France to Wales, thence to England, and part to United States, or more properly, South Carolina; and from this branch all of the name in this country spring.

I have looked carefully into the descent of Miss Marion Thayer Capers, and also of yourself, and you both come from the same family. She is in the direct line from one of three Capers brothers that settled in So. Carolina in [1678?], and you are the offspring of another of these brothers.

Very truly yours,

CATHARINE T. R. MATTHEWS.

Croton-on-Hudson, N. Y., May 18, 1899.

F. L. C.—Capers Family—Pages 18 & 19.

Capers

Azure, three foxes passant; argent in pale.
Over all a crescent argent.
CREST: a bunch of grapes proper.
MOTTO: Perserverentia Vincit   (Perserverance conquers)
Foxes passant represent wit and cunning.

Crests were given for some deed of valor; they were marks of honor.
The crest of Capers, a bunch of grapes, may have been given for some
brave deed in or near a vineyard. The crescent was usually put on the
shield on the top to distinguish the family of the second son. When used
as a charge, it showed that the bearer was a Crusader.
(FLC's booklet on the Capers Family.)

INTRODUCTION

This book had its beginning with a collection of information accumulated in the files of W. M. Capers, Esq., Columbia, South Carolina. Efforts to add to this collection were successful and rewarding. It is, of course, not perfect, but hopefully makes some contribution to the history of this family and the several related families included in this work.

In 1898 the late Francis LeGrand Capers, then of Pueblo, Colorado, employed a reliable genealogist to research the origin of the Capers family and procure the facts on its developments in America. He very generously had this work completed and published in booklet form in 1908.

In 1858 William M. Wightman, D.D., completed and had published a book on the life of Bishop William Capers.

In 1901 the Honorable A. S. Salley, Jr., State Historian, published "Captain William Capers and Some of His Descendants" in the S. C. Historical and Genealogical Magazine. This work is an excellent example of the complete research and detail for which the late Mr. Salley was so highly respected.

In 1912 Walter B. Capers, D.D., having collected many family and Civil War records, published "The Soldier Bishop—Ellison Capers."

On motion of Mr. W. M. Capers the compilation of such records as follows is gratefully dedicated to the memory of these four gentlemen.

According to the records, William Capers, with brothers Richard and Gabriel, came to America about 1680. William appears to have been a man of some means having land grants from the Lords Proprietors. He owned lands on the islands off the coast of South Carolina and lots in the City of Charleston. He was a planter and also a dealer in hides and leather goods. This seems to say that there may have been some connection with the firm of James Capers & Company, an old establishment in Liverpool, England, dealing in such products at that time. For the sake of identity and clarity, this William is designated "Captain William" and sometimes as William I as he was the first by that name in America. He and his family were members of the Church of England and served as vestrymen of Christ Church in that parish of South Carolina beginning in 1708 or before.

In the case of brothers Richard, a planter, and Gabriel, a school teacher, the historical indications are that their lines of descent established the "Sea Island Capers" around Beaufort, South Carolina, and extended later to other parts of the South.

Every effort has been made to avoid errors. Hopefully none have been made but some may possibly have occurred. Please be assured that such will be regretted. We have done the best we could with the data available and hope that the information compiled will, at least, be helpful to those who would improve on this work in the future.

There have been several by the name of William Capers. It is, therefore, in order to designate as follows:

William I was the first by that name in America. He is referred to in colonial records as Captain William Capers. Richard I was brother of William I. Richard II was son of William I.

Bishop William was a bishop of the Methodist Episcopal Church (South).

Major William or "The Major" was a Major of Militia after the American Revolution. During that contest he was first a Lieutenant in the Continental Army. He was transferred to General Francis Marion and served as one of his captains. He is referred to as Captain William Capers as well as "The Major," which title came after the war.

Bishop Ellison was Ellison Capers I. Brig. Gen. CSA and later Episcopal Bishop of S. C.

Bishop William T. or "W. T." was William Theodotus Capers who was a son of E. C. I and became Episcopal Bishop of West Texas.

Ellison Capers, Jr. (1869-1918) is referred to as Ellison Capers II for the purpose of clarification. He was a son of Bishop Ellison Capers.

C. T. R. Matthews, Genealogist, reported in 1899 that she had found in the possession of Miss Marion Thayer Capers, Crystal Springs, Mississippi, the seal of her great great grandfather and indicating that he was Gabriel I, the school teacher immigrant.

According to a letter from Mrs. W. H. Johnson (Lottie Palmer Capers) her friend and cousin Thayer Capers, wife of Admiral Allen, Commandant Charleston Navy Yard in 1942 advised that her father was an Episcopal minister from New Orleans and that her grandfather was Richard Farr Capers.

Unfortunately, she did not give her father's name. The name THAYER, however, is so unusual that it is a fair guess to say that that Miss Marion Thayer Capers and Mrs. Thayer Capers Allen were of the same line of descent. Latter's daughter was Miss Thayer Capers Allen.

Francis LeGrand Capers I (1853-1919) in his booklet in 1908 mentions at page 25 Thomas Farr Capers, as a descendant of Gabriel I.

So the inclusion of the name FARR for both Richard and Thomas seems to support this theory.

(WMC—1972)

Major GABRIEL CAPERS of Christ Church Parish was the son of Richard II and grandson of William I. He was the uncle of Major William and Captain George Sinclair, brothers who fought in the American Revolution. Major Gabriel had daughters but no sons. He was foster father to the two nephews named and did well by them. This Gabriel was a member of the first and second Provincial Congress and the S. C. General Assembly.

Another Gabriel Capers was a brother of Bishop William. He moved to Louisiana and died at Ocean Springs, Miss., in 1867.

John Singletary Capers (1792-1862) was also a brother of Bishop William. A descendant was William Henry Capers, an Episcopal Minister in Mississippi probably father or grandfather of Dr. Gerald Capers of Tulane University, New Orleans.

(WBC 1950)

A guess would be that the following might be correct.
1. John Singeltary (1792-1862)   m. Martha White
2. William   m. Sarah English
3. John Singeltary
4. William Henry
5. Dr. Gerald Mortimer

(WMC 1972)

LeGrand Guerry Capers, another brother of Bishop William, served in the War of 1812 on General Worth's staff (JAG). His daughter Sarah married General Swift. His son Dr. LeGrand Guerry Capers, Jr. was a Surgeon in the Confederate Army. Another son was Francis LeGrand who was the first in the Francis LeGrand Capers line.

(WBC 1950 & WMC 1972)

NOTES

Barnwell, So. Carolina, Nov. 16th, 1899.
Mrs. J. R. Matthews,
Croton-on-Hudson, N. Y.

My Dear Madam: Your favor bearing date of 14th inst. is before me, and I take pleasure in giving you what information I can.

I cannot tell you anything of the origin of the name of Capers. As regards my connection with that family will say, my father's grandmother was a Miss Anna Rowe, of Orangeburgh, So. Ca., and her mother was a Miss Ladson, of St. Helena Island, S. Ca., who married Mr. Gabriel Capers (a school teacher). Said Mr. Gabriel Capers came direct from England, (I think about 175 years ago). He left England, I have been told, because his father, (name unknown) desired him to take Holy Orders, to avoid which he came to this country. There are still some Capers on St. Helena's Island, who no doubt could give you the desired information.

The above information I received from my father, Rev. Wm. Otis Prentiss, (who departed this life last Sept., aged 83).

If at any time I can be of any service to you, please call upon me.

Yours very truly,

S. E. PRENTISS.

F. L. C.—Capers Family—Page 15

Pueblo, Colo., Dec. 4, 1907.
Mr. Henry D. Capers, 907 Austell Bldg., Atlanta, Ga.

My Dear Cousin: In further answer to your esteemed favor of the 29th. There are a few things in regard to our genealogical tree that I want to call your special attention to, all arguments to the contrary notwithstanding. In the first place your family name was Capier, and this name was not changed until our people left France. In the second place, while it is true that we are of English descent, the original stock came from Flanders. And it is also true that we are Hugenots. The above you want to remember.

I took the question up of finding out who I was some 10 years ago, and I thought it would cost me maybe $50.00 or $100.00, and before I got through I spent way over $1000.00. And I hunted down the family in France, England and this country thoroughly, and therefore the facts that I give you are absolutely correct; and the arms and crest are likewise correct . . .

Your affectionate cousin,

FRANK

F. L. C.—Capers Family—Page 24.

CHRIST CHURCH RECORDS

The Parish Register of old Christ Church furnishes us with the most convincing evidence that the Capers who founded the family in South Carolina were not only identified with the Colonial Church, but were also prominent officials in that historic parish. Christ Church is six miles from Mount Pleasant, near Charleston, and is one of the eight parishes established by act of Assembly in 1706. The present building was erected after the Revolution, the original church having been burned by the British. Some years before the first church was erected the following record appears in the parish register: *

BIRTHS

May 6th, 1696. Mary, daughter of William Capers and Mary his wife.

December 15th, 1698. William, son of William and Mary Capers.

June 5th, 1701. Elizabeth, daughter of William and Mary Capers.

April 28th, 1712. Richard, son of William and Mary Capers.

BAPTISMS

June 8th, 1729. Mary, daughter of Thomas and Mary Capers.

MARRIAGES

January 9th, 1741. Richard Capers and Elizabeth Bouhoist, spinster.

January 3rd, 1753. Peter Leguieu and Amerlia Capers, widow.

BURIALS

April 28th, 1720. Mary Capers, widow.

July 15, 1739. Ann, wife of Richard Capers.

March 18th, 1739. Mary Capers.

In the days of the Colonial Church the common law required wardens and vestrymen to take the oath of office. We find one William Capers subscribing to the oath as warden, 1708, 1709, 1712, and again in 1717 and 1718, and Richard Capers II, son of William, taking the same oath in 1736.

---

* The church was completed 1706.
THE SOLDIER-BISHOP, pp 21-22.

1790 CENSUS OF SOUTH CAROLINA

(First U.S. Census)

BEAUFORT DISTRICT

Head of family	Males 16 & older	Males under 16	Females	Slaves
Cha Capers	3	I	2	45
Wm Capers	I	–	I	15
Rach Capers	I	3	2	8

CHARLESTON—CHRIST CHURCH PARISH

Gabrial, Capers	I	–	8	82
George Capers	I	4	I	15

CHARLESTON—ST. THOMAS PARISH

Wm. Capers	2	2	3	29

NOTE: Copied verbatim including name abbreviations.

TABLE OF CONTENTS

WILLIAM CAPERS I LINE (C)

CAPTAIN WILLIAM CAPERS I, married MARY ————, apparently MARY DuBOSE, b. 16—, d. 1720, who married in 1695. She was dau. of Isaac DuBose, Huguenot emigrant to South Carolina from Dieppe, France and wife, Suzanne Couillandeau, of La Tremblade, Saintonge, France. Capt. William d. about 1718.

C-1. Mary, b. May 6, 1696, m. (1) John Simes who d. Aug. 1716; m. (2) Oct. 1717, Thomas Boone, who d. Nov. 2, 1749. By her first husband she had (A) Mary, b. Jan. 13, 1715 and (B) Sarah Simes, b. Aug. 20, 1716 who m. Jan. 30, 1737, James White, M.D. A son, James was buried Oct. 9, 174–. (Christ Church Records.)

C-2. William, b. Dec. 15, 1698, predeceased his father.

C-3. Elizabeth, b. June 5, 1700, d. 1733, m. as his first wife, Col. George Benison who d. June 9, 1748. He m. (2) in 1735, Hannah Screven, wid. His will made in Christ Church Parish (1747), Berkeley County, S. C., gentleman, mentions son William to whom he leaves land called "Youghall," next to Capt. Thomas Boone; sons, Richard d. ca 1758, in this state and George, Jr.; "brother" Richard Capers who was also named executor; daughters, Elizabeth; Jane; Sarah who m. James Parris in 1742 and their children Peter and Elizabeth Parris; Mary who m. William Gibbes, sadler, in 1744 and had Mary Gibbes, then under age 18. "Youghall" named after a place in Ireland. Original grant, 1696.

George Benison, Jr., b. 1722, m. Elizabeth Bremar, will dated Apr. 7, 1751, and had Wm. and Francis Bremar Benison. He d. intestate ca. 1750. William, son of Geo. Sr. m. Ann Brown in 1750 and d. 1751.

C-4. Sarah, b. Apr. 5, 1701.

*C-5. Richard, b. April 28, 1712, d. ca. 1774, m. three times.

C-5. RICHARD CAPERS, 2 (Wm. 1), m. (1) May 17, 1730, ANN SINCLAIRE who d. July 15, 1739, m. (2) Jan. 8, 1741 ELIZABETH BONHOSTE, who apparently died without issue. Elizabeth was the dau. of Jonas Bonhoste, Jr. and Elizabeth Bacot. Richard m. (3) Aug. 2, 1744, MARY ANN DUPUY MAYBANK, wid. of Joseph Maybank. No issue but she had 5 children by her first marriage.

Issue by first wife only:

C-6. Elizabeth, b. Oct. 3, 1731.

C-7. William, b. Nov. 26, 1732, d. bef. 1774, m. Dec. 4, 1753, Catharine Dutarque, dau. of Capt. John Dutarque, of the parish of St. Thomas and St. Denis. One son, William, b. 175–, d. unmarried between May 7, 1779 and Nov. 28, 1785.

*C-8. Richard, b. ca. 1734, m. Martha Bordeaux.

*C-9. Gabriel, b. 173–, of St. Thomas Parish m. (1) Martha Witherston of Charles Town, spinster, and (2) Sarah Lloyd.

C-8. RICHARD CAPERS, 3 (Richard 2, Wm. 1), m. ca. 1755, MARTHA BORDEAUX. Probably died before 1774.

*C-10. Major William, m. (1) Mary Singeltary, m. (2) Mary Wragg and m. (3) Mrs. Hannah (Coachman) Postell.

C-11. George Sinclair, d. 1809, Sumter District, S. C., Captain of militia and State regulars. On one occasion led one of Marion's scouting parties of 12 men into St. Thomas's Parish where they encountered a party of 26 British Black Dragoons and cut them to pieces.

C-9. GABRIEL CAPERS, 3 (Richard 2, Wm. 1), m. (1) Nov. 1767, MARTHA WITHERSTON who d. Sept. 1776; m. (2) Nov. 11, 1777, SARAH LLOYD of Charles Town, who d. Mar. 26, 1808. Gabriel d. ca. 1800.

C-12. Catherine, m. Hugh Paterson and died Mar. 30, 1808.

C-13. Mary, d. unm. Oct. 21, 1812.

C-14. Martha, m. Nov. 29, 1810, Hugh Paterson, merchant, who had first married her sister Catherine.

C-15. Sarah, m. 1806, David Jervey, M.D.

C-16. Elizabeth, 1789-1852, m. Maurice Simons, 1790-1836, son of Maurice Simons II and wife, Elizabeth, neé Simons. No issue.

C-10. MAJOR WILLIAM CAPERS, 4 (Richard 3, 2, Wm. 1), b. St. Thomas's Parish, Oct. 13, 1758, m. (1) Sept. 10, 1783, MARY SINGELTARY, b. Nov. 6, 1766, d. March 1792, dau. of John and Sarah Singeltary of the vicinity of Cainhoy "Wando." William m. (2) Nov. 11, 1793, MARY WRAGG, of Georgetown, b. 1767, d. Feb. 7, 1801, dau. of Samuel Wragg and Judith Rothmahler, granddau. of Joseph Wragg, of His Majesty's Council in S. C. and Judith DuBosc, dau. of Marie DuGué and Jacques DuBosc, merchant of Charleston. Jacques was son of André DuBosc of St. Ambrose in Languedoc, France, and wife, Marie LeStoade.

William Capers of Waccamaw m. (3) May 15, 1803, MRS. HANNAH (COACHMAN) POSTELL, widow of Col. Jehu Postell, at "Rural Hall" near Georgetown. William d. at his plantation, Sumter Dist., Dec. 7, 1812.

Issue by first wife, MARY SINGELTARY.

C-17. Sarah, b. 1784, m. (1) LeGrand Guerry and (2) The Rev. John B. Glenn.

*C-18. Gabriel, m. Ann Humphries.

C-19. Mary Singeltary, d. young.

*C-20. The Rt. Rev. William, b. Jan. 26, 1790, d. Jan. 29, 1855, Bishop of Methodist Ep. Church, South, m. (1) Anna White and (2) Susan McGill (Magill).

*C-21. The Rev. John Singeltary, m. Martha E. White.

Issue by second wife, MARY WRAGG.

*C-22. The Rev. Samuel Wragg, b. Mar. 5, 1797, m. (1) Elizabeth Humphries; m. (2) Sarah M. Brandt, and m. (3) Abathiah Harvey Thornton.

C-23. Elizabeth, d. young.

C-24. Mary.

C-25. Henrietta.

Issue by third wife, MRS. HANNAH COACHMAN POSTELL.

*C-26. LeGrand Guerry, m. (1) Abigail Swift and m. (2) Amelia Freelove Layton.

C-27. The Rev. Benjamin Huger, Methodist minister, married and moved to Mississippi. Issue.

C-28. Richard Coachman.

C-18. GABRIEL CAPERS, 5 (Wm. 4, Richard 3, 2, Wm. 1), m. ANN HUMPHRIES, dau. of the Rev. Thomas Humphries, of Jeffer's Creek, Darlington District, S. C.; d. Ocean Springs, Miss., 1867.

C-29. The Rev. Thomas Humphries, Methodist minister, m. in St. Louis, Mo., Miss ——— Hamilton. Died Monticello, Florida. Issue: (A) James Hamilton, m. and had a son and a daughter, Luna, who m. the Rev. Howard Sledd of Virginia, (B) William, lived Richmond, Va. and (C) Ella, who married and lived in Georgia.

C-30. Eliza, m. ca. 1827, George Whitfield Ellis and died ca. 1897. Issue.

C-31. Mary Singeltary, b. 1815, m. in Macon, Ga., 1831, Benjamin R. Warner, of Connecticut. Issue: (A) A. Lou, d. July 1897, ae 83, m. in 1856, Horace E. Walpole and had (a) Kate Seymour who m. F. Y. Legaré and (b) Horace E. Walpole, who m. Miss A. J. Hay. (B) Benjamin Warner, lived Johns Island, S. C. Six other children but no record.

C-32. Wesley Coke, C.S.A., fought in War with Mexico.

C-33. Susan, d. unm.

C-34. Gabriel, farmer, married and had issue.

C-35. Robert Francis Withers, m. but no issue.

C-36. The Rev. Stephen Olin, Methodist minister.

C-37. John Singeltary, farmer, m. but died without issue.

C-20. THE RT. REV. WILLIAM CAPERS, 5 (Wm. 4, Richard 3, 2, Wm. 1), b. on his father's Bull's Head plantation, St. Thomas's Parish, Charleston District., S. C., Jan. 26, 1790. Educated at Dr. Roberts' academy, near Stateburg, Sumter Dist. and at S. C. College. Married (1) Jan. 13, 1813, ANNA WHITE, b. Feb. 20, 1795, only dau. of John White, Esq. of Georgetown Dist., S. C., deceased, and wife, Anna. Anna d. Dec. 30, 1815 and he m. (2) Oct. 31, 1816, SUSAN McGILL, or MAGILL, b. Aug. 31, 1797, dau. of William and Ann McGill from Ireland but then of Kershaw Dist., S. C., adopted dau. of Mrs. Peter Hörry, wid. of Gen. Peter Hörry.

Issue by first wife, ANNA WHITE.

C-38. Anna White, b. Jan. 18, 1814, m. Dec. 23, 1830, the Rev. William Holmes Ellison.

C-39. Theodotus William, b. Dec. 30, 1815, d. Nov. 16, 1816. His mother died at the time of his birth.

Issue by second wife, SUSAN McGILL.

C-40. Francis Asbury, b. Dec. 26, 1817, d. Jan. 10, 1818.

*C-41. Francis Withers, b. Savannah, Ga., Aug. 8, 1819, m. (1) Hannah Hawk Bascom and m. (2) Susan Rutledge.

C-42. Susan Bethia, b. Mar. 11, 1821, Savannah, Ga., m. July 23, 1843, Professor George Washington Whitfield Stone, b. Nov. 28, 1818.

C-43. Esther Anslie Withers, b. Dec. 7, 1822, d. Oct. 15, 1824.

C-44. The Rev. Dr. William Tertius, b. Milledgeville, Ga., Jan. 20, 1825, Methodist minister, m. (1) Dec. 20, 1853, Lucy Frances Austin, dau. of William L. M. and Elizabeth Austin; m. (2) Sarah Bell; died Sept. 10, 1894, bur. Columbia, S. C. No issue.

C-45. Sarah Ann Branham, b. Jan. 13, 1827, Charleston, S. C., m. Jan. 2, 1849, William Montague Sage, b. Aug. 27, 1824, of Charleston, S. C. No issue.

C-46. Harriet Emma Maria Haslope, b. Charleston, S. C., July 31, 1830, d. July 11, 1855, m. Aug. 8, 1848, the Rev. Samuel Barksdale Jones, b. Dec. 29, 1828, distinguished Methodist minister, son of Thomas Legaré Jones, b. Charleston, 1800 and Emeline Fishburne. Issue: (A) Susan Barksdale, b. Aug. 18, 1849; (B) Sarah Elizabeth Whitner, b. Feb. 28, 1853 and (C) William Capers Jones, 1851-1854.

C-47. Mary Singeltary, b. Charleston, S. C., June 28, 1833, m. 1855, the Rt. Rev. Peter Fayssoux Stevens.

*C-48. Henry Dickson, b. June 2, 1835, Columbia, S. C., m. Mary Elizabeth Means.

*C-49. The Rt. Rev. Ellison, named for his brother-in-law, the Rev. William Holmes Ellison, D.D., b. Oct. 14, 1837, m. Charlotte Rebecca Palmer, 1837-1908.

C-50. Theodotus LeGrand, b. Oct. 23, 1839, Charleston, S. C., grad. with first honors in his class at college, June 1860, killed at 2nd Manassas, Aug. 30, 1862, Sgt., C.S.A.

C-21. THE REV. JOHN SINGELTARY CAPERS, 5 (Wm. 4, Richard 3, 2, Wm. 1), b. 1792, d. of malarial fever, Georgetown, S. C., 1862. Methodist minister. Married MARTHA E. WHITE whose will was probated Feb. 17, 1863.

C-51. John Singeltary, Jr., d. bef. 1863. His mother's will mentioned that she was left to act as his Executrix.

C-52. Annie, m. Josiah Doar. Issue. No mention of her is made in her mother's will.

C-53. Eliza Henrietta, m. Gabriel Capers Jervey.

C-54. William, m. Sarah English and had (A) Mary, (B) Ansley, (C) Mittie, (D) John Singeltary.

C-55. Sarah Eliza, d. age 7 mo., bur. Capers-Guerry Cemetery.

C-56. Sarah Crawford, d. age 7 days, bur. Capers-Guerry Cemetery.

C-22. THE REV. SAMUEL WRAGG CAPERS, 5 (Wm. 4, Richard 3, 2, Wm. 1), b. Georgetown Dist., S. C., Methodist minister, m. (1) May, 1817, ELIZABETH W. HUMPHRIES who d. ae 19, Mar. 29, 1818; m. (2) Oct. 1826, SARAH M. BRANDT, and after her death, m. (3) Jan. 11, 1831, ABATHIAH HARVEY THORNTON, who was living in 1900 in Camden, S. C. Died Jan. 22, 1855, bur. Camden, S. C.

*C-57. Samuel Elizabeth, 1818-1874, m. Sophia Vogan Reynolds.

Issue by second wife, SARAH M. BRANDT.

C-58. Margaret, d. age 3.

Issue by third wife, ABATHIAH HARVEY THORNTON, daughter of Phineas Thornton and Elizabeth Williams, of Raynham, Mass.

*C-59. Richard Thornton, m. Mary Hard (or Hurd).

C-60. Abathiah Elizabeth, m. Dr. F. L. Zemp.

C-61. Edmund LeGrand, d. in infancy.

C-62. Sidney Williams, m. (1) Jessie Lee Darby and (2) in 1874, Edith Wightman, who d. 1886, dau. of Bishop William May Wightman and wife Edith.

C-63. John Summerfield, killed at Appomattox Court House, April, 1865, age 23.

C-64. Mary Wragg, b. 1844, m. the Rev. Christopher Thomasson and had (A) Mary, who d. age 3, (B) John Summerfield who d.y., (C) Samuel Capers Thomasson. Mrs. Mary Capers Thomasson gave material on the family for *Historic Camden* in 1926.

C-65. Sarah Ann Gamewell, b. 1846, m. the Rev. A. J. Stokes, D.D., Methodist minister and had (A) Lalla Capers who m. the Rev. W. C. Kirkland, (B) Emma J. D., (C) The Rev. (M.D.) Whitefoord J. Stokes, b. Spartanburg, S. C., April 6, 1865.

C-66. Caroline Martha Michel, 1848-1890, n.m.

C-67. Emma Jane Dunlap, 1850-1878, m. James Nelson of Kershaw County, S. C. and had (A) Abathiah Harvey Nelson who m. A. Wineberg.

C-68. Edwin Benjamin, 1852-1901, n.m.

C-69. Adella Henrietta, d. inf.

C-26. LeGRAND GUERRY CAPERS, 5 (Wm. 4, Richard 3, 2, Wm. 1), b. Sept. 15, 1808, Sumter Dist., S. C., d. Brooklyn, N. Y., Jan. 29, 1868, bur. Manhassett, L. I.; m. (1) June 1, 1829, ABIGAIL SWIFT, Oct. 16, 1810-Aug. 30, 1846; m. (2) April 27, 1851, in San Antonio, Texas, AMELIA FREELOVE LAYTON, b. Aug. 20, 1814, near Roslyn, L. I., d. Sept. 9, 1907.

Issue by first wife, ABIGAIL SWIFT.

C-70. Abigail, m. —— Swift.

C-71. LeGrand Guerry, Jr., M.D., Confederate Surgeon, d. Vicksburg, Miss. Issue.

C-72. John Edwards, living in 1908.

C-73. Martha Glover, m. Richardson Cornwall Layton.

C-74. Richard Coachman.

C-75. Sarah, m. General Swift, U. S. Army.

C-76. Child who d. young.

C-77. Child who d. young.

*C-78. William Worth, b. Aug. 30, 1844, m. Ella Ferguson.

C-79. Child who d. young.

Issue by second wife, AMELIA FREELOVE LAYTON.

C-80. Amelia Freelove, m. J. Lefferts Thorn of St. John, New Brunswick, Canada.

C-81. Josephine Wright, m. Ammi V. Young of Berlin, Germany.

*C-82. Francis LeGrand, b. May 21, 1853, Roslyn, L. I., N. Y., m. June 3, 1880, Emma M. Cole, of Brooklyn, N. Y.

C-83. Mary Cornwall, m. Henry M. Newton of Yarmouth, Me., lived in Montclair, N. J. in 1908.

C-41. FRANCIS WITHERS CAPERS, 6 (Wm. 5, 4, Richard 3, 2, Wm. 1), d. 1892, Charleston, S. C., m. (1) Aug. 24, 1848, HANNAH HAWK BASCOM, dau. of Alpheus and Cassandra Bascom, of Ky. She d. Jan. 20, 1862 and he m. (2) Jan. 1, 1863, SUSAN RUTLEDGE of Charleston, S. C., dau. of John Rutledge and Maria Rose. Susan d. 1901.

Issue by first wife only:

*C-84. William Bascom, b. Dec. 19, 1849, m. April 3, 1879, Caroline Bosworth Sibley, of Augusta.

*C-85. Francis Withers, Jr., b. July 13, 1852, m. Henrietta Fannie Clark.

C-86. Alpheus Bordeaux, b. July 6, 1855.

C-87. Emma Singeltary, b. July 21, 1856.

C-88. Mary Percival, b. Apr. 26, 1858, d. July 24, 1858.

C-89. Clara Stewart, m. Dr. Lawrence B. Owens.

C-48. HENRY DICKSON CAPERS, ESQ., 6 (Wm. 5, 4, Richard 3, 2, Wm. 1), attorney in Atlanta, Ga., b. 1835, Columbia, S. C., m. in Oxford, Ga., Oct. 20, 1857, MARY ELIZABETH MEANS, 1835-1885, dau. of Dr. Alexander Means. Died in 1912. Author of *Belleview, Life and Times of C. G. Memminger* and many newspaper and magazine articles. Appointed Chief Clerk and Disbursing Officer, Treasury Dept., C.S.A. under the Hon. C. G. Memminger, Sec. of the Treasury. After the capital was moved to Richmond he resigned and entered the Confederate Army. He was a Colonel of Cavalry, C.S.A. at the end of the war. See: Recollections of the Civil Service of the Confederate Government (1887).

Dr. Alexander Means, b. 1801, d. Oxford, Ga., 1883, pioneer in scientific education, minister, teacher and scientist, one of the founders of Emory College (Oxford), served a brief time as its president.

C-90. Alexander Means.

C-91. Minnie Eloise, 1859-1933, m. in 1881, Bedford McKinney Harlan, 1850-1924, and had Sue Harlan who m. (1) ——— Trammell and (2) G. J. Jernigan. She was b. in Calhoun, Ga., member of Colonial Dames (1936) having William Capers as her ancestor.

C-92. Charles Memminger.

C-93. Theodotus LeGrand.

C-94. William.

C-49. THE RT. REV. ELLISON CAPERS, 6 (Wm. 5, 4, Richard 3, 2, Wm. 1), b. Oct. 14, 1837, d. Columbia, S. C., Apr. 22, 1908. May 4, 1893, was unanimously elected bishop of the Diocese of South Carolina, Protestant Episcopal Church. On Feb. 24, 1859 married CHARLOTTE REBECCA PALMER.

C-95. Catherine Marion, b. at The Citadel, Charleston, S. C., Mar. 2, 1860, d. in infancy.

C-96. Francis Fayssoux, b. The Citadel, June 5, 1861, d. Dec. 16, 1911, educated Patrick School, Greenville, S. C., Carolina Military Academy, and University of the South, Sewanee, Tenn., m. Jan. 27, 1885, Emma Maxwell (Emmala) Keels, of Greenville, S. C., no issue. She m. (2) James Whittemore of Santa Barbara, Cal. He was named for his uncles Francis Capers and Peter Fayssoux Stevens. Buried Christ Church (Episcopal), Greenville, S. C.

C-97. Susan McGill, b. Columbia, S. C., Nov. 11, 1862, d. in inf.

C-98. Mary Videau Marion, b. Oxford, Ga., July 17, 1864, m. Capt. Charles Boothe Satterlee.

*C-99. John Gendron Palmer, named for his maternal grandfather but later dropped "Palmer," b. April 11, 1866, m. (1) Susan Keels, sister of Emmala who m. his brother, and after her death m. (2) Lilla Trenholm.

*C-100. The Rt. Rev. William Theodotus, Episcopal Bishop, West Texas, b. Aug. 9, 1867, m. (1) Rebecca Holt Bryan and (2) Mrs. Louis Cash.

*C-101. Ellison, b. May 9, 1869, d. Dec. 30, 1918, Summerton, S. C., m. Carlotta Manigault Benbow.

*C-102. The Rev. Walter Branham, Episcopal minister, b. 1870, m. Louise Drane Woldridge, d. 1952.

C-103. Charlotte Palmer, b. Aug. 12, 1871, d. Feb. 21, 1960, m. May 5, 1898, Dr. William Henry Johnson, of Charleston, S. C.

C-57. SAMUEL ELIZABETH CAPERS, 6 (Samuel 5, Wm. 4, Richard 3, 2, Wm. 1), m. Dec. 20, 1837, SOPHIA VOGAN REYNOLDS, dau. of Dr. Joshua Reynolds of Ireland, teacher and druggist; granddau. of the Rev. Samuel Mathis, first male born in the town of Camden, S. C. who married Margaret C. Miller.

C-104. George, 1854-1880.
*C-105. William Reynolds, 1854-Jan. 17, 1901, m. Jennie Allen, 1856-1934.
C-106. Samuel Wragg, 1852-1877.
C-107. Francis Vogan, 1857-1923, m. Sarah Cornelia Elizabeth Mc-Fall and had (A) Francis Vogan, Jr., d. inf., (B) Sophia V., d. inf., (C) Samuel, d. inf., (D) Mary McFall, d. 1951, (E) Eleanor E., d. 1962, (F) Cornelia Reynolds, d. 1971, m. Percy Richmond and had (a) Robert who m. Marion Portzer and had (1) Bruce and (2) Clive Richmond who in 1972 m. Nancy Puglise. (G) Ruth Winifred (d. 1972) who m. Matthew W. Renfrette, Esq., of Washington, D. C., and had (a) Kay Elizabeth Renfrette, b. Sept. 29, 1939.
C-108. Margaret, 1849-1904.
C-109. Elizabeth W., 1838-1841.

C-59. THE REV. RICHARD THORNTON CAPERS, 6 (Samuel 5, Wm. 4, Richard 3, 2, Wm. 1), m. MARY HARD. He was a Methodist minister.

C-110. Maynie Harvey.
C-111. John Swinton.
C-112. Annie, m. Clifton Harvey.
C-113. Sidney.
C-114. Helen.

C-78. WILLIAM WORTH CAPERS, 6 (LeGrand 5, Wm. 4, Richard 3, 2, Wm. 1), m. June 26, 1867, ELLA FERGUSON, b. Oct. 17, 1848.

C-115. William Worth, Jr., b. 1868.
C-116. Louis, b. 1869.
C-117. Linda Dalavar, b. 1872.
C-118. Ella Maude, b. 1873.

C-119. Grace Ferguson, b. 1877.

C-120. Edna Mitchell, b. 1878.

C-121. Marcia Ferguson, b. 1879.

C-122. Mabel Swift, b. 1881.

C-123. LeGrand, b. 1883.

C-82. FRANCIS LeGRAND CAPERS, 6 (LeGrand 5, Wm. 4, Richard 3, 2, Wm. 1), m. EMMA M. COLE, dau. of David Cole, of Chicago, Ill. Author of booklet on Capers family printed in 1908. Died 1919.

*C-124. Francis LeGrand, Jr., b. Mar. 14, 1884, d. 1937, graduated Harvard College, June, 1907, m. Ethel Davis, b. 1887.

C-84. WILLIAM BASCOM CAPERS, 7 (Francis 6, Wm. 5, 4, Richard 3, 2, Wm. 1), b. Dec. 19, 1849, Transylvania College, Lexington, Ky., where his father was professor of ancient languages and literature, m. Apr. 3, 1879, CAROLINE BOSWORTH SIBLEY, b. near Augusta, Ga., June 21, 1859, d. Aug. 29, 1896. She was dau. of Edward Amory Sibley and Sarah A. P. Wheeler, granddau. of Amory and Caroline B. Sibley and Nathan and Lydia (Pendelton) Wheeler. William d. Augusta, Ga., age 66. All issue born Augusta, Ga.

C-125. William Bascom, Jr., b. Mar 16, 1880, d. age 33.

C-126. Sarah Augusta, b. May 4, 1882, d. age 25.

*C-127. Frank Bascom, b. Oct. 15, 1884, m. (1) Theresa Geibner and (2) Willa Waddey Hirschman, of Augusta, July 10, 1929; d. May 18, 1930, Gracewood, Ga.

C-128. Edward Amory, 1887-1887.

C-129. Charles Sibley.

C-130. Caroline Doughty, b. Aug. 22, 1896, m. Thomas Bruton Rountree, Mar. 20, 1924, Augusta, Ga., d. Jan. 23, 1972, Augusta. Issue: (A) Thomas Bruton, Jr., b. Jan. 5, 1925, d. Jan. 8, 1925. (B) Sarah Caroline, b. May 5, 1926, North Augusta, S. C., m. (1) Marshall Norris Rosier, July 3, 1947 and had (a) Marshall Norris, Jr., b. Dec. 12, 1949. Dvd. and m. (2) Carl Brinson, Feb. 28, 1959, and had (b) Constance Lombard, b. Oct. 10, 1959 and (c) Susan Capers Brinson, b. Feb. 22, 1963. (C) Richard Capers, b. North Augusta, Aug. 1, 1927, m. Martiel Ellison, Nov. 20, 1954 and had (a) James Richard, b. Oct. 26, 1955, Augusta (b) Thomas David, b. Nov. 12, 1957, Augusta (c) Ronald Ellis, b. Jan. 17, 1961, Greenville, S. C. and "Debbie" Rountree.

C-85. FRANCIS WITHERS CAPERS, JR., 7 (Francis 6, Wm. 5, 4, Richard 3, 2, Wm. 1), m. June 1, 1885, HENRIETTA FANNIE CLARK, b. Aug. 31, 1855, dau. of the Rev. Dr. James Osgood Andrew Clark, b. Savannah, Ga., Oct. 8, 1827, d. Macon, Ga., and wife, Amanda Augusta Mann, dau. of John H. and Henrietta Ann Mann.

C-131. Marian Bascom, b. April 4, 1886, d. Jan. 4, 1920, n.m.

*C-132. Francis (Frank) Withers, b. June 5, 1887, m. June 2, 1921, Lisa Fargo who was b. Dec. 10, 1889, d. Oct. 23, 1971.

C-133. Ruth Clark, b. Oct. 13, 1888, d. July 3, 1944, n.m.

C-134. Osgood Clark, b. Feb. 16, 1890, d. July 14, 1891.

*C-135. Anderson Clark, b. Dec. 6, 1892, d. May 30, 1970, m. June 24, 1920, Louise Stebbins, b. Mar. 12, 1895.

C-136. Emma Jane, Dec. 12, 1893-Dec. 2, 1896.

C-137. Myra D'Antignac, Feb. 25, 1895-Feb. 16, 1896.

C-138. Rutledge Mann, b. June 2, 1899, d. Aug. 16, 1932, m. April 26, 1924, Lucille Arrington. No issue.

C-99. JOHN GENDRON CAPERS, ESQ., 7 (Ellison 6, Wm. 5, 4, Richard 3, 2, Wm. 1), b. "Box Cottage," Anderson, S. C., Apr. 17, 1866, educated Patrick's School, Holy Communion Church Institute, S. C. Military Academy; admitted to S. C. bar, 1887. Married (1) Dec. 1888, SUSAN KEELS, dau. of John Keels and Martha Maxwell, who d. March 1890, without surviving issue; m. (2) June 18, 1895, LILLA TRENHOLM, of Charleston, S. C., granddau. of George Trenholm, Secretary-Treasurer, C.S.A., and dau. of Francis Holmes Trenholm and first wife, Mary Elizabeth Burroughs.

John was assistant U. S. Attorney, Dept. of Justice, 1895-1901; appointed U. S. District Attorney for S. C., July 24, 1901. Collector Int. Revenue, U. S., Washington, D. C. Died Sept. 5, 1919.

C-139. John Ellison, d. age 4 mo.

Issue by LILLA TRENHOLM.

C-140. Charlotte Palmer, b. Dec. 24, 1896, m. Sept. 1, 1920, Major-Gen. U.S.M.C., Ralph Stover Keyser, from Va. He is now deceased. Their first child died at birth and they adopted her nephew Francis Frederick Towers whose mother died at the time of his birth, Jan. 28, 1913. Issue of Charlotte and Ralph Keyser: (A) Charlotte Capers Keyser, ("Kitsey"), m. (1) Chauncey Brewster Chapman, Jr., in 1945, and had (a) Chauncey Brewster III, b. 1949, (b) Rebecca Palmer, b. 1952 and (c) Susan Keyser Chap-

man, b. 1957. Charlotte m. (2) Berrien Eaton and had (d) Anne
Berrien Eaton, b. 1962.

C-141. John Gendron, Jr., b. March 22, 1898, d. Mar. 26, 1899.

C-142. Frances Trenholm, m. Frederick N. Towers, Esq., and had
(A) Francis Federick Towers, Lt., USMCR, W.W. II, killed at
Iwo Jima.

C-143. John Gendron (II), b. June 3, 1910, called "Jack", Lt. Col.
W.W. II, USMCR, 3rd Gen., Citadel, Charleston, S. C., m. Mary
Bliss Fine and had (A) John Gendron III, b. June 30, 1943, m.
Ann Reed Bateman, 1972, (B) Rushton Trenholm, b. Nov. 2, 1945,
m. Christine Scott Shumate, 1968, and had (a) Mary Scott Capers,
b. Mar. 15, 1970. Mary Bliss Fine is the dau. of Andrew Mellick
Fine, descendant of pre-American Revolution Dutch settlers,
Martin L. Fine and Larnella Chambers. Her mother was a dau.
of Valentine Bliss who came from England in 1879 and m. Mary
Ann Rushton.

C-100. THE RT. REV. WILLIAM THEODOTUS CAPERS, 7 (Ellison
6, Wm. 5, 4, Richard 3, 2, Wm. 1), b. at the Rectory, Greenville,
S. C., Aug. 9, 1867, d. 1943, educated Furman University, S. C.
College, and Virginia Theological Seminary; m. (1) REBECCA
HOLT BRYAN, of Augusta, Ga., Jan. 30, 1889, dau. of General
Goode Bryan, of Augusta, and m. (2) MRS. LOUIS CASH. Named
by his father for his two brothers William and Theodotus, killed
in War Between the States. William was elected Bishop of West
Texas (Episcopal).

C-144. Bryan, d. inf.

*C-145. Ellison Howe, b. June 1, 1892, m. Margaret Baylor Van
Meter, Dec. 29, 1915.

*C-146. The Rev. William Theodotus, Episcopal minister, b. June
3, 1895, Sumter, S. C., d. July 16, 1954, Tryon, N. C., m. (1)
Ruth Logue Morton and (2) Doris Mary Wiles.

C-147. The Rev. Samuel Orr, b. Anderson, S. C., Aug. 2, 1899,
sometime rector of Christ Episcopal Church, San Antonio, Texas,
m. Eleanor Stribling.

C-101. ELLISON CAPERS II, 7 (Ellison 6, Wm. 5, 4, Richard 3, 2, Wm.
1), originally named Ellison Palmer Capers but dropped the "Palmer"
and became Ellison Capers, Jr., m. June 9, 1892, CARLOTTA
MANIGAULT BENBOW, b. June 25, 1875, d. 1951, of Clarendon
County, S. C. She m. (2) ERNEST J. ROBERTSON.

C-148. Ellison III, b. Apr. 15, 1893, d. 1933, m. Catherine Rice, dau. of Capt. Samuel M. Rice and Annie M. Morrall, 1st Lt., W.W. I. Issue: (A) Ellison IV, LCDR, USN (Ret.) b. Nov. 10, 1921, m. Betty Black, dau. of Joseph Benjamin Black and Margaret Moore, and had (a) Ellison V, b. April 21, 1952 and (b) Marcia Lofton, b. May 26, 1954, (B) Samuel Rice ("Kip"), b. Oct. 27, 1928, d. 1958.

C-149. Emmala Frances, b. Jan. 1, 1895, m. William Capers James, Brig. Gen. USMC (Ret.), son of Joseph Alston James, 1866-1937, who m. in 1890, Wilmington, N. C., Mary Rivers Evans, 1868-1952, dau. of Capt. John Jacob Evans, b. Cumberland, Md. who m. Mildred Holmes, dau. of Owen Holmes and Sarah Lovick Black. Issue: (A) Emmala C., m. Feb. 10, 1943, Dr. James Allan Graham, of N. Y., and had (a) Sarah Stewart, b. Aug. 18, 1945, and her twin, Mary Capers, b. 1945 and (c) James Allan Graham, Jr., b. Apr. 26, 1955. (B) William Capers James, Jr., b. Jan. 31, 1923, Lt. Col. USMC (Ret.), m. Peggy Rule and had (a) Rule Capers, b. Nov. 25, 1950, (b) William Capers, b. Dec. 4, 1952 and (c) Kristen Charlotte James, b. Apr. 18, 1956.

C-150. Katherine Marion, b. Summerton, S. C., May 7, 1897, m. George Duncan Lesesne of Mobile, Ala. and had (A) Katherine Capers Lesesne, b. Feb. 18, 1924.

C-151. William Manigault, Esq., b. July 16, 1905, m. 1930, Helen DuBose, dau. of John Bratton DuBose and Kitty Rion. Dvd. No issue. Graduate University of S. C. and University of S. C. Law School, W.W. II, LCDR, USNR.

C-102. THE REV. WALTER BRANHAM CAPERS, 7 (Ellison 6, Wm. 5, 4, Richard 3, 2, Wm. 1), b. at the Rectory, Greenville, S. C., Aug. 8, 1870, educated Furman University, S. C. College, and Virginia Theological Seminary. Named for a kindly Methodist minister, the Rev. Walter R. Branham, of Oxford, Ga., who aided Charlotte Palmer Capers and her small children to escape the Union invaders. See *Soldier Bishop*. In Columbia, Tenn., June 29, 1904, m. LOUISE DRANE WOLDRIDGE, dau. of Dr. Walter Parrish Woldridge and Eliza Jane Keesee, b. Jan. 8, 1884, Columbia, Tenn., d. Jackson, Miss., Jan. 14, 1961. He d. Oct. 11, 1952, Jackson, Miss. Issue: (A) Walter Woldridge, b. Nov. 23, 1905, Columbia, Tenn., d. Dec. 13, 1938, m. Emily Keith Frazer, dau. of Henry Shelby Frazer and granddau. of Walter Keith. No issue. Attorney, Dean and Senator. (B) Charlotte Palmer, b. June 28, 1913, Columbia, Tenn., historian, sometime Director of Archives, State of Miss.

C-105. WILLIAM REYNOLDS CAPERS, 7 (Samuel 6, 5, Wm. 4, Richard 3, 2, Wm. 1), m. JENNIE ALLEN, in 1877.

C-152. E. Allen, M.D., 1879-1925, m. in 1905, Eula Lee Drummond. Issue: (A) Harold Drummond, 1908-1956, m. in Texas 1932, Ruth Starke and had (a) Olivia, b. 1936, (b) Carolyn, b. 1937, and Mary, b. 1944. (B) William A., m. Juanita Bruton, in N. C. in 1935, and had (a) William A., Jr., b. 1948 and (b) Richard Michael, b. 1950. (C) Edward Allen, b. 1915, m. Josephine Philson, 1941, Columbia, S. C. and had (a) Edward Allen, Jr., b. 1943, m. in 1967, Greta Shealy Ward, (b) Adelaide, b. 1947, m. James Edward Johnson in 1972. (D) Francis Ralph Capers, b. 1918, not married in 1973.

C-124. FRANCIS LeGRAND CAPERS, JR., 7 (Francis 6, LeGrand 5, Wm. 4, Richard 3, 2, Wm. 1), m. ETHEL M. DAVIS.

*C-153. Francis LeGrand III, b. 1914, m. 1935, Caretta Elizabeth Miles. He is president of McKesson-Robbins Drugs, N. Y.

C-154. John Davis, m. (1) Annabel Johnson and (2) Eleanor Laaker and had (A) Judith V., b. 1943, m. John Robert Daniel and had (a) Judith Daniel.

C-155. Richard Guerry, 1927-1963, m. Clair De Foreit and had (A) Gary Davis Capers, b. 1959.

C-127. FRANK BASCOM CAPERS, 8 (Wm. 7, Francis 6, Wm. 5, 4, Richard 3, 2, Wm. 1), m. (1) THERESA GEIBNER and (2) WILLA WADDEY HIRSCHMAN.

C-156. William Bascom, b. 1913, m. Mable Clair Herndon, April 17, 1941, North Augusta, S. C. She was b. Apr. 13, 1924, Powelton, Ga., dau. of Mary Eliza Cooper and William Newton Herndon, d. May 18, 1973, Augusta, Ga. Issue: (A) Minnie Carolyn, b. Aug. 16, 1943, Augusta, Ga., m. James Barry Baggott, Nov. 14, 1963, b. Apr. 26, 1943, in North Augusta, S. C., and had (a) James Barry, Jr., b. July 22, 1967 and (b) Scott Capers Baggott, b. Oct. 31, 1969, both b. Augusta, Ga. Minnie Carolyn furnished information on this branch of the family. (B) Patricia Jean, b. Dec. 19, 1950, Augusta, Ga., m. May 8, 1971, in North Augusta, Donald Edward Beall, b. Sept. 26, 1952, (C) Mary Clair, b. Augusta, Ga., Sept. 26, 1952.

C-157. Clara, n.m.

C-158. Christine, m. James Herman Watkins and had James Herman, Jr.

C-132. FRANCIS (FRANK) WITHERS CAPERS III, 8 (Francis 7, 6, Wm. 5, 4, Richard 3, 2, Wm. 1), lives Augusta, Ga., m. LISA FARGO.

C-159. Francis (Frank) Withers IV, Esq., b. Sept. 22, 1922, m. (1) Sept. 12, 1949, Sally Carrere Bussey, Augusta, Ga., b. Oct. 1927, d. July 4, 1952; m. (2) Martha Strickland, b. Oct. 30, 1932. He furnished information on this family. Issue by first wife: (A) Sallie Carrere, b. Nov. 27, 1950, m. Aug. 12, 1972, Clyde Warner Jordan, b. June 6, 1948, son of Mr. and Mrs. Hoyt Jordan, of Savannah, Ga. Issue by Martha Strickland: (B) Frank Withers V, b. Jan. 2, 1958 and (C) Lisa Bryson, b. Mar. 3, 1959.

C-160. John Davison, b. Feb. 29, 1924, m. June 27, 1952, Margaret Sherman, b. Apr. 22, 1931. Issue: (A) John Davison, Jr., b. May 17, 1953, (B) Mark Verdier, b. Oct. 2, 1955 and (C) Margaret Sherman, b. Jan. 31, 1958.

C-135. ANDERSON CLARK CAPERS, 8 (Francis 7, 6, Wm. 5, 4, Richard 3, 2, Wm. 1), m. LOUISE STEBBINS.

C-161. Marian Bascom, b. Sept. 3, 1921, m. Aug. 11, 1942, Milledge Peterson, b. May 18, 1920. Issue: (A) Milledge, Jr., b. Aug. 27, 1943, m. Sept. 6, 1969, Patricia Wilder, b. Mar. 23, 1948, (B) Alice Louise, b. Aug. 12, 1946.

C-162. Frances Stebbins, b. May 11, 1923, m. Aug. 17, 1942, Augusta, Ga., William Innis Bouton, of Ware Shoals, S. C., b. July 9, 1918. Issue: (A) William Innis, Jr., b. May 14, 1944, d. Jan. 9, 1969. (B) Margaret Collins, b. Feb. 7, 1947, m. Oct. 14, 1967, Kenneth Craig Ketcham and had (a) Frances Parrott and (b) Margaret Ann Ketcham. (C) Ralph Rothery, b. Dec. 17, 1948, m. June 17, 1972, Rebecca Carpenter. (D) Capers, b. Oct. 2, 1950. (E) Charles Leonard, b. June 18, 1952. (F) Henry Cagle, b. June 29, 1958 and (G) Robert Collins Bouton, b. Sept. 11, 1962.

C-163. Anderson Clark, Jr., b. May 10, 1925, m. Oct. 7, 1949, Emily Smith, b. Aug. 30, 1925. Issue: (A) Anderson Clark III, b. Aug. 19, 1951 and (B) Mary Louise, b. Mar. 11, 1965.

C-164. Stewart Gregory, b. May 12, 1929, m. Mar. 29, 1952, Angel Allison, b. July 15, 1931. Issue: (A) Stewart Gregory, Jr., b. Feb. 25, 1953. (B) Marian Allison, b. Oct. 18, 1954. (C) Thomas Edward, b. Dec. 31, 1955. (D) Phillip Barfield, b. Aug. 7, 1961. b. June 25, 1963.

(E) Stephen Rutledge, b. Dec. 7, 1958 and (F) Carolyn Clifford,

C-145. ELLISON HOWE CAPERS, 8 (Wm. 7, Ellison 6, Wm. 5, 4, Richard 3, 2, Wm. 1), named by his father, Bishop William T. Capers, for two bishops, Bishop Ellison Capers and his predecessor, Bishop William Bell White Howe, 6th Bishop of South Carolina, Episcopal Church. Ellison m. MARGARET BAYLOR VAN METER, b. May 19, 1894, Lexington, Ky., dau. of Solomon Lee Van Meter and Evelyn Trent Swoope, of Stanton, Va.; granddau. of Solomon Van Meter and Martha Prewitt; and George Washington Swoope, Jr. and Margaret Baylor; great-granddau. of Isaac Van Meter and Rebecca Cunningham; and George Washington Swoope and Eliza Trent; great-great-granddau. of Jacob Van Meter and Tabitha Inskip; and Jacob Swoope and Mary McDowell. The Van Meter line goes back to the founding of Augusta County, Va., 1730, by John Lewis from Ireland.

> C-165. Ellison Van Meter, M.D., b. Mar. 30, 1919, m. Rose Marie Doherty, b. June 22, 1925. Issue: (A) Ellison Douglas, b. Sept. 6, 1946. (B) Kathleen Margaret, b. July 6, 1950. (C) Jeffrey Philip, b. April 12, 1952, d. Apr. 5, 1961. (D) Christopher William, b. Aug. 1, 1955 and (E) Rose Marie, b. Jan. 6, 1963.

> C-166. Baylor Van Meter, b. June 7, 1921, m. Eleanor Vail, b. May 29, 1923. Issue: (A) Alice Lucile, b. July 27, 1952. (B) Jane Vail, b. Jan. 4, 1953. (C) Eleanor Joane, b. Dec. 14, 1954 and (D) Baylor Van Meter, Jr., b. June 1, 1960.

> C-167. Margaret Van Meter, m. Joseph Rich Proctor, Jr., b. April 29, 1923. Margaret was b. May 31, 1928. Issue: (A) Margaret Van Meter, b. Sept. 4, 1952. (B) Rebecca Howe, b. Feb. 25, 1955. (C) Evelyn Swoope, b. June 14, 1956. (D) Daniel Rich, b. Mar. 7, 1958 and (E) Jennie Hamilton Proctor, b. July 28, 1961.

C-146. THE REV. WILLIAM THEODOTUS CAPERS, JR., 8 (Wm. 7, Ellison 6, Wm. 5, 4 ,Richard 3, 2, Wm. 1), m. (1) in 1921, RUTH LOGUE MORTON, dau. of James Austen Morton. She died in 1922 and he m. (2) June 12, 1927, DORIS MARY WILES, of London, Eng., dau. of William Henry Wiles, 1870-1920, and Elizabeth Emma Crabb, 1869-1957. Ordained priest in June, 1927 (Episcopal Church), served churches in San Antonio, Okmulgee, Okla., Terre Haute, Ind., St. Michael's, Charleston, S. C. and last in Tryon, N. C. where he died.

> C-168. Ruth Bryan, b. Feb. 27, 1922, m. John Frasar Austen who d. in 1956. In 1972 she was living in Infanta, Quezon, Phillipines. Issue by DORIS MARY WILES.

C-169. William Theodotus III, b. Oct. 3, 1928, m. Oct. 4, 1954, Mrs. Susanna M. (Johnston) Traylor who had a son by her previous marriage, Patrick Nicholas Traylor, b. July 26, 1949. In 1973, William was Lt.-Col., USAF, Director of Information for Civil Air Patrol. Issue: (A) Rebecca Johnston, b. 1955. (B) Catherine Ann, b. 1956. (C) Melissa Mary, b. 1964.

C-153. FRANCIS LeGRAND CAPERS III, 8 (Francis 7, 6, LeGrand 5, Wm. 4, Richard 3, 2, Wm. 1), m. CARETTA ELIZABETH MILES, b. 1911, dau. of Walter Richard and Elizabeth Kirk Miles, of N. C.

C-170. Francis LeGrand IV, m. Virginia Davis, b. 1946, dau. of Joseph and Ann Davis.

C-171. Ann Elizabeth, b. 1941, m. Donald R. Freiday, son of Donald and Marjorie Freiday. Issue: (A) Robert Walter, b. 1965 and (B) Catherine Ann Freiday, b. 1969.

C-172. Catherine May, b. 1943, m. Stephen Abbott Fairfield, son of Paul A. and Deleanor Dexter Fairfield and had (A) Parker Abbott, b. 1969 and (B) Derek Fairfield, b. 1971.

(*The News and Courier*, Mon., March 8, 1971, Charleston, S. C.)

HOUSE IS UNDERGOING THIRD RENOVATION

By W. H. J. THOMAS
Staff Reporter

The large Georgian dwelling house at 69 Church St., probably the city's earliest surviving residence of mansion proportions to have a symmetrical "double house" floor plan, is at present being renovated extensively for the third time since its construction more than 225 years ago.

This current renovation by its present owners, Mr. and Mrs. Anthony Cecil, is an attempt at genuine restoration, a term much used in Charleston while less frequently achieved. The Cecils have set about the remodelling of a much-changed dwelling of national importance with the goal of restoring many of the Georgian details which have been lost through changes in fashion and destruction by war and natural disasters.

The house stands on property owned by Capt. William Capers as early as 1715. Capt. Capers, progenitor here of an English family of uncertain French origin, died in 1718, and the land in time passed to his youngest son, Richard Capers (1712-1774), who as an adult became a properous Christ Church Parish planter.

The Church Street lot was securely his by 1745 and it was about this time that he apparently built this large home, perhaps as a wedding gift for his recently acquired third wife, the former Mary Ann Maybank.

To judge from construction details uncovered during the current remodeling, Capers built a residence with four rooms to each of its three stories plus full-height attic. In typical double house manner, the entrance floor was in four evenly proportioned rooms with a center hallway as divider from east wall to west. Both second and third floors had three rooms of equal size with large sitting rooms to the southeast corner taking in the area of the hallway to the east side so that these had a three-bay front.

Because of the size and weight of this house, an inner framing construction was created to carry all of this rather than simply using a straight baring-wall method. In the basement, the builder placed two massive rows of brick piers which ran from front to rear on the lines of the hallway, with 14-by-14 beams resting on these.

Cross joists were placed on these beams, studs rising then to additional parallel 15-by-14 timbers, with another row of upright studs rising on the second story to a single 12-inch-by-36-inch beam which supported the weight of third and fourth floors. This plan may best be described as a reverse small "h" rising up two and one half stories if seen directly from the Church Street side looking west.

Because of a slight dip in the roof line where the front gable joins the main truss work, it appears that this house originally had a hip roof and the pediment and stucco consoles were a later addition.

The dwelling later became the residence of Col. Jacob Motte, public treasurer of the Royal Colony, and then was purchased in 1778 by James Parsons, wealthy lawyer and planter. From 1800 to 1811, the house was owned by a planter and merchant named O'Brien Smith and it is Smith who probably made the first remodeling by replacing most of the cornices with examples from the Adam style, adding mantles of a fashionable design. He repaneled several of the rooms with low-relief Adam details, including all the little applied putty swags in the dado band of the first floor rear library.

Smith sold this house, six plantations (Duhanon, Litchfield, Youghall, Prospect, Chickees and Dungannon), numerous slaves and livestock to John Pyne for $200,000. Pyne lived on here until his death in 1821 when the property went to his widow and half-dozen other heirs. It was held by the heirs until 1866, and probably during the 1840s, under their ownership, the house was once again remodeled.

There is some question about this matter, but it seems in the ante-bellum period the center door was changed to the far north front bay, a dining room was thrown open across the rest of the first story front (requiring the removal of the 14-by-14 beam on the south between first and second floors). The second story drawing room was expanded full across the front (requiring the removal of most of the wall beneath the 12-by-36 inch top beam).

In 1869, the house was sold to Mrs. William Mason Smith. Her descendants were to retain the property for 100 years, among these being her son, Daniel Elliott Huger Smith, who with his own distinguished daughter, Alice Ravenel Huger Smith, the noted watercolorist, wrote the "Dwelling Houses of Charleston."

The Cecils found the ante-bellum project had so weakened the reverse "h" support framing that the great 12-by-36 beam had cracked badly and the general structure was sagging. Closing in the floor plan to its original arrangement has not only given it back its Georgian aspect but created the necessary stability as well.

While much of the Adam detail is being retained, the Greek revival features have been removed and proper paneling and classical entablatures added to the principal rooms. The Cecils made an additional discovery when several Adam mantles were removed for repairs; beneath these were found the old blue Dutch chimney tiles from the early 18th century. Forty of them were saved and another 360 ordered from a firm in Holland, which still makes them, to be placed in four fireplace openings.

BOONE FAMILY (B)

MAJOR JOHN BOONE, b. ca. 1645, will proved Aug. 25, 1711, son of THOMAS I and SARAH BOONE, came to S. C., ca. 1673, received a large grant of land east of the Cooper River. Was Lord Proprietor's Deputy, member of Grand Council; married ELIZABETH PATEY, dau. of THEOPHILUS PATEY and they were founders of Boone Hall Plantation.

    *B-1. Capt. Thomas, b. 1690, d. 1749, Justice of Peace, m. Mary Capers Simes, wid. of John Simes, dau. of William Capers I.

    B-2. Theophilus, under age Nov. 8, 1706 when father made will as being from Berkeley County, gentleman.

    B-3. Elizabeth, m. (1) Mark Holmes and (2) Francis Croxton.

    B-4. Susannah, m. George Haddrell.

    B-5. Sarah, m. Nov. 2, 1723, Capt. Hugh Hext.

    B-6. Mary, underage in 1706.

B-1. CAPT. THOMAS BOONE married MARY (CAPERS) SIMES, wid.

    B-7. John, b. Feb. 24, 1719/20, bur. Dec. 15, 1721, Christ Church.

    *B-8. Thomas, b. Nov. 4, 1723, d. 1784, m. Nov. 23, 1741, Susannah Croft, b. June 22, 1724, dau. of Edward Croft and Elizabeth Brewton; granddau. of Col. Miles Brewton who d. in 1745 and his first wife, name unknown. Col. Brewton came to S. C., age 9, with parents, July 12, 1684, a goldsmith and banker, Capt. of one of the two militia companies in Charles Town.

    B-9. Susannah, b. Jan. 9, 1726, m. (1) in 1740, Richard Beresford; m. (2) in 1742, Hugh Hext, and (3), May 14, 1745, the Rev. Levi Durand.

    B-10. William, b. Apr. 12, 1728, d. 1775, m. Mary Croft.

    B-11. Capers, b. Aug. 23, 1732, m. (1) Catherine Croft, m. (2) in 1767, wid. Mrs. Mary Smith who d. Nov. 1777; and m. (3) in 1779, Mary Boyd, spinster. He was member of 2nd Provincial Congress of S. C.

    B-12. Patey, b. June 16, 1730, d. July 7, 1739, one of set of twins, other still born.

    B-13. John II, b. Oct. 9, 1734, d. Jan. 6, 1777, Christ Church.

B-8. THOMAS BOONE, of Prince Frederick Parish, m. SUSANNAH CROFT.

    B-14. Thomas, b. 1745, m. in 1769, Hannah Atkinson and had (A) Martha, b. 1779 and probably others.

B-15. John, b. 1755, d. Feb. 8, 1792, m. in 1776, Sarah Gibbes and had (A) John Gibbes, (B) Sarah, (C) James, (D) George, (E) Susan, (F) Maria Glover who m. George Fraser, (G) Thomas who m. Mary Jones, (H) Susan (II), b. Jan. 20, 1789, d. Oct. 25, 1864, m. in 1810, Henry Alexander DeSaussure.

B-16. Susannah, m. 1768, John Gaillard, son of Alcimus Gaillard and his second wife, Elizabeth Gendron.

B-17. Peter, b. 1760.

B-18. James, b. 1763, m. 1785, Sarah Blake.

WILL OF MARY CAPERS SIMES BOONE, of Christ Church Parish, Berkeley, (S. C.), dated Sept. 2, 1780, probated Nov. 24, 1780, names her grandsons, Thomas and John Boone as executors. Mentions:

Sons, Thomas, William and Capers.

Grandsons, Thomas, son of Thomas
William, son of William
Capers, son of Capers
John, son of Thomas

Residue of estate to Sims White

Granddaughters, Mary Croft
Lydia Boone, under 21 and unmarried
Susannah Gaillard
Mary White, dau. of James White
Sarah Boone, under 21 and not married

Great Grandsons, Alcimus Gaillard
Thomas Boone
Sims White, under 21 and not married, son of grandson Sims White
John White, son of grandson Sims White

Great Granddaughters, Mary White, under 21 and not married, dau. of Sims White.
Mary Gibbes, under 21 and not married
Elizabeth Gibbes, under 21 and not married.

DeSAUSSURE FAMILY (De)

HENRY ALEXANDER DeSAUSSURE, b. Sept. 15, 1788, d. Dec. 9, 1865, m. Dec. 18, 1810, SUSAN BOONE, dau. of JOHN and SARAH (GIBBES) BOONE. Both bur. Congregational Church (Circular), Charleston, S. C.

De-1. Sarah Gibbes, m. (1) 1832, Alexander L. Baron and (2) Stephen Elliott.
*De-2. Henry William, M.D., m. 1840, Mary Coffin Peronneau.
De-3. Wilmot Gibbes, m. 1846, Martha Gourdin.
De-4. Louis Daniel, m. 1847, first cousin, Sarah Martin DeSaussure.
De-5. Susan M., m. 1852, R. S. Screven.

De-2. HENRY WILLIAM DeSAUSSURE, M.D., m. MARY COFFIN PERONNEAU, b. 1821, dau. of Henry William Peronneau, b. 1793, d. Mar. 28, 1858, who m. Mary Coffin, b. 1798, d. 1864.

De-6. Dr. Henry William, Jr., b. Feb. 28, 1847, m. Mary Broün Sinkler, b. 1845, dau. of Margaret Huger and James Sinkler, granddau. of William Sinkler of Eutaw Plantation and Elizabeth Allen Broün. Issue: (A) Meta, (B) Henry who m. Margaret Whittaker, (C) Nannie and (D) Elizabeth Allen DeSaussure.
De-7. Mary Coffin, m. the Rev. Innis LaRoche.
De-8. William Peronneau, m. Georgiana S. Logan.
De-9. Alexander Baron, of Charleston, m. his cousin, Ida Champion DeSaussure, in 1870, dau. of Major John McPherson DeSaussure of Camden, S. C. who m. Eliza Hester Champion in 1832, dau. of Richard L. Champion and Mary Louisa DuBose. Major J. M. DeSaussure was a son of Chancellor Henry William DeSaussure.
De-10. James Peronneau, b. Mar. 25, 1853, d. Dec. 23, 1895, m. Oct. 28, 1879, Annie Isabella Laurens, who d. Apr. 19, 1919.
De-11. Amory Coffin, d. y.
De-12. Susan Boone, m. Benjamin L. Owens.
De-13. Elizabeth, m. George Tucker.

DuBOSE FAMILY (Db)

ELIZABETH CAPERS ZEMP, b. 1884, m. THE REV. PALMER CLISBY DuBOSE, son of the Rev. Hampden Coit DuBose, D.D. of Darlington, S. C., 1845-1910, and Pauline McAlpine, of Talladega, Ala., 1850-1914, dau. of Dr. A. I. McAlpine and Martha Clisby, of Boston; granddau. of the Rev. Robert McAlpine of Union, Tenn., later of Ga. Dr. DuBose was a pioneer Southern Presbyterian missionary to China.

Db-1. Clisby Blakeney, b. Jan. 3, 1907.

Db-2. Eugene Zemp, b. Oct. 1, 1910, Soochow, China, m. Oct. 16, 1937, N. Y. City, Virginia Watson Smith, b. June 1, 1907, Port Chester, N. Y., dau. of Hay Watson Smith and Jessie Rose, and had (A) Eugene Zemp, Jr., b. May 30, 1942, N. Y. City, m. April 11, 1971, Cranford, N. J., Marcia Ruth Rubine, b. Plainfield, N. J., June 27, 1945, dau. of George Adolph Rubine and Vera Carolyn Newmark. (B) Cynthia E., b. Apr. 22, 1948.

DuPRÉ FAMILY (D)

The DuPré family left France after the Revocation of the Edict of Nantes, 1685, went to England, then came to Carolina, in 1686. JOSIAS, the emigrant, was probably the son of SAMUEL, who d. in Carolina before 1695, and was buried at Pompion Hill Churchyard. Josias and his wife, MARTHA, found Benjamin Simons in England and brought him with them to Carolina. He later married their daughter, Mary Esther. Josias was granted land in the Orange Quarter in 1702.

D-I. JOSIAS and MARTHA ————.

D-II. JOSIAS II and SARAH GARNIER, dau. of Daniel and Elizabeth (Fanton) Garnier of the Isle de Re, near La Rochelle, France.

D-III. JOSIAS GARNIER and ANN BLAKE (?).

D-IV. DANIEL and MARY NORMAND.

D-V. SAMUEL and MARY STEED ALLSTON, dau. of Josias and Esther Simons Allston of Turkey Hill Plantation, Waccamaw (S. C.).

D-VI. DANIEL and SARAH MARGARET HIBBEN, dau. of James and Margaret Wells Hibben. One son, Warren had son Daniel Allston DuPré who m. Helen Capers Stevens, dau. of Bishop Stevens and Mary Capers.

D-VII. JOHN YOUNG, M.D., m. (1) MARY REBEKAH JERMAN and (2) ELIZA ANN ALLSTON JERVEY. Dr. DuPré, b. July 2, 1827, was surgeon in local Coast Guards, assistant surgeon in siege of Petersburg. He d. Feb. 21, 1900 and his wife, Eliza Jervey, three days later.

D-1. Daisy, d. inf.
D-2. Esther.
D-3. Twin to Esther, Susan, d. inf.
D-4. John Palmer, M.D., b. Dec. 7, 1872, m. Apr. 30, 1907, Mary Coleman, of Laurens, S. C., and had (A) Mary Allston, (B) John Coleman, (C) Andrew Hibben, (D) Emmie Chicora and (E) Robert Quillen DuPré.
D-5. Samuel Jervey, b. Nov. 9, 1873, d. Apr. 5, 1957, m. Jan. 7, 1908, Hallie Mathews, of Montgomery, Ala., and had (A) Eloise Mathews, (B) Samuel Jervey, Jr., (C) Emily Mathews, (D) John Young, (E) Charles Henry and (F) Lila Lindsay.

D-6. Gadsden Maybank, d. inf.

D-7. Emily Courtenay, b. 1878, m. 1902, Lee Royall and had (A) John Edward, (B) Emily DuPré, (C) Sarah Hibben, (D) Lee, (E) Anne Bailey, (F) Jervey DuPré and (G) Susan Allston Royall.

DURAND FAMILY (Du)

THE REV. LEVI DURAND, Episcopal minister m. (1) CHAR-
LOTTE ———— who d. Oct. 10, 1744 and was bur. in chancel under
the altar of Christ Church. They had a son, Levi, who was baptised
Oct. 8, 1744 and a daughter, Susanna, who died Aug. 29, 1745. LEVI m.
(2), May 14, 1745, SUSANNAH BOONE, dau. of MARY CAPERS and
THOMAS BOONE.

The Rev. Durand, of St. John's Parish, Berkeley Co., mentions in
his will, dated Mar. 16, 1765, probated May 17, 1765, his wife, Susannah,
and sons, also sons' grandfather, Capt. Thomas Boone. "The money I
have in England is to remain at interest for my sons, library books are
to be divided between my wife and five children." John Boone and
Peter Bacot, a Charles Town merchant, were executors.

The Rev. Durand had been rector of Christ Church Parish for 11
years when invited to take over St. John's Parish, Berkeley, on Aug. 28,
1750. In 1761 he went "to the Northward" with the Rev. Mr. Garden,
Rector of St. Thomas'. Constant residence in the country and the heavy
duty of the missions were blamed for his death.

Du-1. Levi, b. Dec. 25, 1746, wit. the will of Peter Singellton (sic),
St. Stephen's Parish, planter, Jan. 7, 1764.

Du-2. Thomas, b. July 16, 1748.

Du-3. James.

Du-4. Mary.

Du-5. Susannah II, m. Joseph Wigfall, Esq., of St. James Santee
and had son Levi Durand Wigfall who was m. by the Rev. Mr.
Jenkins Levi Durand Wigfall, Nov. 4, 1802, to Eliza Thomson,
second dau. of James Hamden Thomson, schoolmaster, who m.
Elizabeth Martha Trezevant in 1775. Levi and Eliza had Hamden
Wigfall who left S. C. College when a Sophomore, 1821-1822.

ELLISON FAMILY (El)

El-I. WILLIAM of Ireland.

El-II. COL. ROBERT, b. County Antrim, Ireland, 1742, came to America ca. 1744, d. Mar. 8, 1806, Fairfield County, S. C., Major in American Rev. under Gen. Moultrie and was Washington's official escort during the President's visit to S. C. 38th Reg't, Brigade IX. Commanding officer of S. C. Militia, 1794. First Warden of Mt. Zion Society, m. (1) Nov. 6, 1772, Elizabeth Potts, b. ca. 1750, Ireland, who d. Jan. 15, 1793. She was mother of his issue.

El-III. JOHN, b. Mar. 8, 1777, d. Dec. 20, 1863, bur. Talbot County, Ga., m. (1) Susannah Milligan, 1779-1817, dau. of Joseph Milligan and Margaret Byers.

El-IV. THE REV. WILLIAM HOLMES, D.D., b. Dec. 4, 1805, Charleston, S. C., d. Dec. 26, 1884, Ala., bur. Meth. Ch. Cem., Clayton, Ala., m. (1) Anna White Capers, b. 1814, d. Mar. 19, 1857, Chunnenuggee, Ala., and m. (2) Mary Jane Oliver Lumpkin, wid. No issue.

William was a grad. S. C. College, 1823, professor and distinguished Methodist minister, President of Wesleyan Female College, Macon, Ga., 1841——, Pres. Chunnenuggee Female College later. Reared a Presbyterian but became a Methodist.

El-1. William Capers, b. Nov. 22, 1831, d. unm.
*El-2. The Rev. John Francis, b. June 1, 1833, m. (1) cousin, Mary Jane Robison and (2) Cornelia Tullis.
El-3. Capt. James Henry, b. Feb. 3, 1836, killed Battle of Gettysburg.
El-4. Susan Anna, b. April 24, 1838, d. ae. 19.
El-5. Julia Margaret, b. Jan. 9, 1841, Macon, Ga., d. May 1906, Cross Plains, Texas, m. Aug. 15, 1865, Jeptha Brantley Carter, at Enon, Ala. They had (A) Henry Ellison, b. 1867, (B) Brantley Persons, b. 1870, (C) Anna Lou, m. Victor White, (D) William Holmes, b. 1873, (E) Jeptha Thadeus, (F) Julia Regina Carter, b. 1876, m. —————— Williamson, Cross Plains, Texas.
El-6. George Pierce, b. Nov. 27, 1843, d. Macon, June 23, 1845.
El-7. Regina Clara, b. Jan. 18, 1845, Macon, Ga., d. Sept. 1, 1917, bur. Clayton, Ala., m. Mar. 12, 1874, Dr. John Thaddeus Floyd, D.D.S., 1847-1930, and had (A) Alice, who m. John Petit West and had (a) John Petit, Jr., (b) Alice Stewart, (c) dau. who

m. A. C. Martin, (d) Regina who m. ———— Mildrum, (B)
Julia Capers who m. Edward Smith, (C) Mary who m. W. T.
Wynne, Milledgeville, Ga. and had W. Wynne, (D) John Thad-
deus who m. Elizabeth Frazier and had John T., Jr., (E) William
Ellison who was b. 1876, d. 1935, m. 1900, Bessie Patterson
Ellison, dau. of Adger Silliman Ellison, 1874-1962, and had (a)
Adger Ellison who m. Inez Thompson, (b) Bessie Robertson
who m. J. W. Hayes and had (1) Bess Hayes, m. D. L. Barton
and had Richard and Susan Terry Barton, (2) Helen Hayes
who m. W. G. Buchanan and had Bill, Brad, Dick and Ann
Buchanan, (c) John Thad, d. inf., (d) Henry Ellison m. and
had Mary and Bill Floyd, (e) William Ellison, d. inf. and (f)
Margaret Terry Floyd who m. Gordon Holmes and had Gordon,
Martha and Betsey Holmes, (F) Florence Floyd, m. Howell
Bentley and had Dale who m. ———— Arner.

El-8. Charles Holmes, b. Oct. 11, 1847, d. age 14.

El-9. Robert Soule, d. young.

El-10. Richard Paine, d. young.

El-11. Alice, d. young.

El-2. THE REV. JOHN FRANCIS ELLISON, b. LaGrange, Ala., d.
Dec. 1868, bur. Union Springs, Ala., m. (1) Nov. 11, 1858, MARY
JANE ROBISON, dau. of the Rev. Winfield Wright Robison of
Columbus, Ga. and Susan Ellison, dau. of John Ellison (El-III) and
Susannah Milligan. She was b. 1840, d. Sept. 1862 and he m. (2)
Cornelia Tullis, b. 1841, dau. of John Richardson Tullis and Lorena
Todd. John taught at Emory College (Oxford) and Chunnenuggee
Female College, Ala. Methodist minister.

Issue by first wife:

El-12. William Winfield, d. Aug. 21, 1861.

*El-13. The Rev. Henry Samuel, b. Mar. 11, 1862, Columbus, Ga.,
d. April 21, 1936, Midway, Ala., m. Emma Clara Hawkins, Nov.
29, 1892.

Issue by second wife:

El-14. John Tullis, Esq., Lawyer and county solicitor, Bibb Co., Ala.
b. 1865, Union Springs, Ala., d. 1947, Centreville, Ala. m. Eva
Lucille Cooper, b. 1879, and had Rhoda Coleman and Cornelia
Tullis Ellison.

El-15. Frances Capers, b. 1867, d. unm. age 24.

El-13. THE REV. HENRY SAMUEL ELLISON, m. EMMA CLARA HAWKINS, b. Oct. 2, 1869, Pollard, Ala., d. Dec. 17, 1965, Montgomery, Ala., dau. of William Henry Hawkins and Nannie Hilburn. Methodist minister.

> El-16. Frances Llewellyn, d. inf.
> *El-17. John Curtis, m. Leone Compton.
> El-18. Mary Emma, m. the Rev. Frank Moore Cross and had (A) Frank Moore, Jr. who m. Elizabeth Ann Showalter and had Susan Elizabeth, Ellen Michiel, and Rachel Patricia Cross, (B) Grace Ellen, who m. Walter Pentz, (C) Robert Laurance who m. Lois Butler and had Robert L., Jr. and Martha Lois Cross.
> El-19. Annie Leigh, m. Adger Ellison King and had (A) Mary Emily, who m. Douglas Hilmar Hassing and had Linda Leigh who m. Robert James Young, Jr.; Douglas Hilmar, Jr. who m. Annette Finney, (B) Virginia Olivia who m. Charles Mitchel Jones and had Charles Mitchel, Jr., (C) Lily Ann King who m. Robert Eugene Keith and had William Adger, Jan Capers, and Olivia Leigh Keith.
> El-20. Lily Cox, m. (1) James S. King and (2) Eric Jeffery Folmar.
> El-21. Julia Capers, m. Frank Gilman White.
> El-22. Henry Samuel, Jr., m. Mae Godwin McCravey and had (A) Henrietta Ellison who m. John Walker Morgan and had John Walker, Jr.

El-17. JOHN CURTIS ELLISON m. LEONE COMPTON.

> El-23. Clara who m. Louis Wilbur Erath. She compiled the book on the Ellison Family which furnished most of the information on this family. Issue: (A) Hulda Louise who m. Gary Russell Weinburger and had Louis Russell Weinburger, (B) Susan who m. Charles Nelson Hutchins and (C) Elizabeth Anne Erath who m. Thomas Alex Bush.
> El-24. Lily Katherine, m. Glenn Clifford Emrick and had (A) Bert Richard who m. Coleen Higgins Linn and had Katherine Elizabeth and Bert Richard Emrick, Jr., (B) Lynne Emrick who m. Douglas Arthur Weaver and had Douglas Arthur Weaver, Jr.
> El-25. John Curtis, Jr., m. Mildred Grace Neal and had (A) Shera Ann who m. Sherwood Clark and had Elizabeth Grace and John Cody Clark, (B) Cynthia Lynn, m. Frank Suggs and had Lisa and Frank Suggs, Jr., (C) Catherine and (D) Annette.

GIBBES LINE (G)

G-I. GOVERNOR ROBERT GIBBES, founder of the S. C. family, came to S. C. from Barbados. He was born in Pandwick, Kent, Eng., Jan. 9, 1644/5, youngest child of ROBERT and MARY (COVENTRY) GIBBES. Gov. of S. C. June 10, 1710-Apr. 2, 1712.

G-II. WILLIAM, b. Feb. 2, 1689, d. Mar. 1733, m. Aug. 2, 1716, Alice Culcheth who d. Aug. 31, 1739.

G-III. JOHN, b. Nov. 12, 1729, d. Dec. 1770, m. (1) Martha Freer. No issue. He m. (2) 1760, Elizabeth White, b. Nov. 15, 1740, dau. of Dr. James and Sarah (Simes) White, of Christ Church Parish.

G-1. Sarah, d. Feb. 16, 1843, m. John Boone. She was great-granddau. of Mary Capers by her first husband, John Simes; John Boone was the grandson of Mary Capers and her second husband, Thomas Boone.

G-2. Mary, d. Jan. 8, 1805.

G-3. Elizabeth, m. Sept. 1784, Robert Boone, 1st cousin of her brother-in-law, John Boone.

GUERRY (GUERRI) FAMILY (Gu)

Gu-I. JACQUES, m. ANNE, "de Sonnet." Lived in Souvet, Poitou, France.

Gu-II. PIERRE I, m. JEANNE BROUSSARD. They are the emigrants to Carolina.

Gu-III. PIERRE II, m. MARGUERITE REMBERT. He was b. in S. C., d. 1736. She was dau. of André Rembert, native of Point en Royan, Dauphin, France, but then of St. James, Santee, Craven.

Gu-IV. PETER I, m. (1) MARY ANNE LeGRAND, d'Anerville, dau. of Isaac LeGrand and m. (2) Judith Rembert Croft, July 30, 1778, Santee, S. C.

Gu-V. PETER II, m. CATHERINE REMBERT, Nov. 12, 1782. He was b. Mar. 13, 1760.

Gu-VI. LeGRAND, b. Sept. 6, 1786, d. 1811, m. SARAH CAPERS, sister of Bishop William Capers.
Gu-1. LeGrand, Jr.
*Gu-2. William Capers, m. Virginia Felder.
Gu-3. LeGrand II.
Gu-4. Sarah Anne.

Gu-2. WILLIAM CAPERS GUERRY m. VIRGINIA FELDER.

Gu-5. William Capers II, 1827-1859, m. in 1855, Caroline Evans and had (A) William Capers III, b. 1857, m. Virginia Ballanger. No issue. (B) Susan Virginia, 1856-1913, m. Felix Carlisle. (C) Caroline Evans, b. 1859, d. unm.

Gu-6. Virginia Galluchet, 1829-1881, m. (1) 1846, Washington Colclough and had (A) Virginia Guerry Colclough. She m. (2) in 1855, Dr. Frederick LaFayette Pride Green, son of Halcott Pride Green, 1821-1891, and Virginia Coles Taylor, 1824-1885, dau. of Benjamin Taylor and Sally Coles. Issue by second marriage: (B) Frederick LaFayette, who m. Eunice Walter, (C) Washington, who m. George Pringle, (D) William Guerry, m. Lilla Kirby, (E) Lucy Jones, m. ———— DeSaussure, (F) Maude, m. ———— Walker. No issue, (G) Allen Cadwallader, 1866-1933, n. m. and (H) Walter Guerry Green, b. 1868, m. Daisy Holt.

Gu-7. John Lawson Felder, 1831-1855, m. Anna Vernon Laney. No surviving issue.

Gu-8. Sarah Capers, b. 1833, m. (1) David Aiken Carson, and (2), in 1855, Edward L. Murray.

Gu-9. Susan McDonald, b. and d. 1835.

*Gu-10. LeGrand Felder, minister Protestant Episcopal Church, m. (1) Serena Margaret Brailsford, dau. of Alexander Baron Brailsford and Anna Eliza James DuBose. He m. (2) in 1871, at Columbus, Ga., Julia Evans and (3) in 1880, Georgia Priscilla Evans.

Gu-11. Walter Capers, 1838-1867, Episcopal minister.

Gu-12. Albert Capers, b. 1840, m. (1) Gertrude Wilson and (2) Ellen Goldsborough Williams. Issue both marriages.

Gu-13. Anna Lawson, 1842-1862.

Gu-14. Mary Irene, 1845-1871, m. ca. 1869, at Florence, S. C., Edward Henry Lucas and had (A) Mary Irene Lucas who m. in 1891, Florence, S. C. Robert Campbell Starr.

Gu-10. THE REV. LeGRAND FELDER GUERRY, 1836-1908, m. (1) Oct. 30, 1860, SERENA MARGARET BRAILSFORD and had:

*Gu-15. The Rt. Rev. William Alexander, Bishop of S. C. Protestant Episcopal Church, 1861-1928, m. Anne McBee.

Gu-16. LeGrand Brailsford, 1862-1871.

Gu-17. Serena Margaret, 1864-1888.

By second marriage, to JULIA EVANS.

*Gu-18. LeGrand, M.D., surgeon of Columbia, S. C., m. Annie Elisabeth Hawkins.

Gu-19. Julia Evans, 1877-1950.

Gu-20. Marie Irene, b. 1874, m. John Joseph Campbell.

Issue by third marriage, to GEORGIA PRISCILLA EVANS.

Gu-21. Georgia Virginia, b. 1881, m. Michael Calhoun Dickson.

Gu-22. Susan Evelyn, b. 1882, m. John McCaw.

Gu-23. Caroline Elizabeth, b. 1884, m. Thomas Keith Legaré.

Gu-24. Walter, b. 1887, m. Lucy Jones Green.

Gu-15. THE RT. REV. WILLIAM ALEXANDER GUERRY, m. ANNE McBEE. He was for 20 years Bishop of the Diocese of S. C. Episcopal Church, b. in Edgehill, S. C., July 7, 1861, d. in Charleston, S. C., June 9, 1928, and is bur. there in St. Philip's churchyard. He m. Nov. 27, 1889, in Lincolnton, N. C., Anne McBee, b. Aug. 5,

1864, Lincolnton, N. C., d. June 5, 1943, in Charleston, also bur. St. Philip's churchyard. She was dau. of Vardry Alexander McBee and Mary Elizabeth Sumner.

Gu-25. Alexander, b. Oct. 17, 1890, Lincolnton, N. C., d. Oct. 19, 1948, m. Dec. 17, 1914, in Chattanooga, Tenn., Charlotte Holmes Patten, dau. of John Patten and had (A) John and (B) Alexander. Alexander Guerry was Vice-Chancellor of Sewanee from 1938 until 1948.

Gu-26. The Rev. Sumner, b. Oct. 6, 1892, Florence, S. C., d. Oct. 3, 1951, Cleveland, Miss., n. m. Priest of Episcopal Church. Missionary to China for five years.

Gu-27. Anne, b. Dec. 25, 1894, Lincolnton, N. C., d. Sept. 20, 1957, in Charleston, S. C., m. in 1916, James Young Perry, b. 1895, Washington, D. C., son of Benjamin Franklin Perry and Ethel Young and had (A) Anne Guerry, b. Jan. 6, 1919, Charleston, S. C., m. Jan. 2, 1942, Hendersonville, N. C., Eldon Durham, b. Sept. 30, 1912, Ashland, Kansas, son of Charles F. Durham and Emma Schooler and had (a) Anne Guerry, b. Feb. 10, 1945, Greenville, Tenn., m. Jan. 30, 1968, Erick Hoddersen (b) Stephen Gaylord, b. Aug. 23, 1947, Hendersonville, N. C. (c) Susan Hayne, b. Oct. 10, 1950, San Pedro, Cal. (d) Hildreth Young Durham, b. July 9, 1953, San Pedro, Cal. (B) James Young, Jr., b. Nov. 19, 1922, Columbia, S. C., m. Mar. 12, 1944, Zirconia, N. C., Llewellyn Atwood LaBruce, dau. of James Bryce LaBruce and Maude Atwood. James, d. Zirconia, N. C., summer of 1965. Issue: (a) Llewellyn LaBruce, b. Zirconia, Apr. 29, 1946, m. Aug. 28, 1968, James Wilson Gibbon Woollcott, son of Corinne Gibbon of Charlotte, N. C., and Philip Woollcott of Asheville, N. C. (b) James Young Perry III, m. Carol Highsmith, Aug. 31, 1969. (C) Ethel Young Perry, b. Oct. 21, 1927.

*Gu-28. The Rev. Moultrie, b. Feb. 12, 1899, Lincolnton, N. C., m. Jan. 21, 1926, St. Michael's Epis. Ch., Charleston, S. C., Elizabeth Robertson Parker, b. Aug. 18, 1901, Charleston, dau. of William Henry Parker and Elizabeth English Robertson.

Gu-29. The Rev. Edward Brailsford, b. Sept. 2, 1902, Atlanta, Ga., m. Feb. 20, 1935, St. Paul's Ep. Ch., Charleston, S. C., Ella Marion Hoffman, b. Sept. 22, 1908, Charleston, dau. of William Gordon Hoffman of Orangeburg, who d. ca. 1933, and Marion Barton Ford, who d. Dec., 1968. No issue.

Gu-18. LeGRAND GUERRY, M.D., b. Feb. 3, 1873, Florence, S. C., d. Aug. 14, 1947, Columbia, S. C., m. July 1, 1899, Augusta, Ga., ANNIE ELISABETH HAWKINS, b. June 23, 1872, Newberry County, S. C., dau. of Benjamin Franklin Hawkins and Alice Eugenia Aughtry. She d. Dec. 31, 1948, Columbia, S. C.

> **Gu-30.** LeGrand, Jr., b. Oct. 30, 1900, Columbia, S. C., d. June 4, 1959, m. Jan. 28, 1922, Nashville, Tenn., Mary Frances Dickerson, b. Jan. 22, 1903, and had (A) Mary Anne, b. Dec. 2, 1923, Nashville, m. 1950, Paul Rodgers, Columbia, S. C. (B) Frances Aline, b. July 6, 1928, Columbia, S. C., m. 1947, Ray Dilly, Columbia (C) LeGrand III, b. Oct. 12, 1935, Columbia, m. June 6, 1959, Pawley's Island, Patricia Mose.
>
> **Gu-31.** Emily, b. Dec. 2, 1903, Columbia, d. Aug. 31, 1971, m. Oct. 30, 1938, Orval Jones, Columbia.
>
> **Gu-32.** Annie Elisabeth, b. Nov. 3, 1908, Columbia, m. Feb. 1, 1929, Walter Monroe Newton.
>
> **Gu-33.** Virginia Felder, b. Feb. 6, 1912, Columbia, m. Oct. 8, 1932, Columbia, John Hardeman Conn who d. Oct. 24, 1958.

Gu-28. THE REV. MOULTRIE GUERRY, m. ELIZABETH ROBERTSON PARKER.

> **Gu-34.** Judge William Moultrie, b. Jan. 7, 1927, Charleston, S. C., m. Aug. 14, 1954, Russell Adelia Bradford, b. Nov. 30, 1932, Norfolk, Va., dau. of Russell Taliaferro Bradford and Jennis Willis Atkinson, and had (A) (dau.) Lee Bradford, b. Jan. 28, 1958, and (B) William Moultrie, Jr., b. Apr. 3, 1961, Norfolk, Va.
>
> **Gu-35.** Sarah Twells, b. Dec. 6, 1930, Sewanee, Tenn., m. June 19, 1954, Roy Anderson Rector and had (A) Elizabeth Twells, b. Aug. 23, 1958, Norfolk, Va., and (B) Roy Anderson Rector II, b. Norfolk, Nov. 23, 1961.

HEXT FAMILY (H)

HUGH HEXT, ancestor of this family, came to Carolina from Dorsetshire, Eng., about 1686. Member of the Commons House of Assembly of the Province in 1706. He had ten children, two being Amias and Hugh, Jr.

H-1. Amias, m. Mary ————, and d. in 1722. His will, dated Feb. 16, 1721, probated Feb. 20, 1723, mentions wife, Mary; sons: Amias and Hugh; daughter: Mary; brother: Hugh, and cousin: Paul Hamilton. His son Hugh, m. Apr. 29, 1742, Mrs. Susannah Beresford, dau. of Thomas Boone and Mary Capers, and wid. of Michael Beresford. Hugh was bur. Oct. 14, 1744. (Christ Church Records.)

H-2. Capt. Hugh, of Colleton County, planter, m. Nov. 2, 1723, Sarah Boone. He d. Nov. 1732 and she m. (2) Andrew Rutledge, attorney-at-law. Hugh's only issue was (A) Sarah who m. Dr. John Rutledge, brother of Andrew Rutledge who married her mother. Dr. Rutledge came to S. C. ca. 1735, m. in 1738.

NOTE: Susan Rutledge who m. Francis Withers Capers, as his second wife, was the dau. of John and Maria (Rose) Rutledge; granddau. of General John Rutledge, b. Charleston, 1766, d. Philadelphia, 1819, member of Congress, 1795-1803, who m. Sarah Motte Smith, 1777-1852, only child of Bishop Robert Smith by his second wife, Sarah Shubrick. General John was the son of John, 1739-1800, and Elizabeth Grimke, and grandson of Dr. John Rutledge who married, 1738, Sarah Hext, 1724-1792. Dr. Rutledge d. Christmas day, 1750, bur. Charles Town, came to S. C. from Ireland with a brother early in the 18th century.

JERVEY FAMILY (JJ)

JJ-I. DAVID JERVEY, founder of the Jervey family of S. C. was a native of Scotland. He came to this state prior to April 5, 1738, for on that date he was married in St. Bartholomew's Parish (S. C.) to ANN DIDCOTT (Dedcott), of Savannah, Ga., but of St. Bartholomew's when married by the Rev. Mr. Archibald Stobo. David was a house builder. In 1773, Ann was a widow, and 50 years of age.

JJ-II. THOMAS JERVEY, m. July 22, 1770, GRACE HALL, dau. of William Hall, of Charleston. Thomas was acting Deputy Muster Master General in the Rev. War, Capt. in S. C. Line, Continental Establishment. Later was a broker and commission merchant in Charleston. After his death, June 14, 1796, his widow m. (2) Thomas Gordon and died on Sullivan's Island, S. C., Sept. 13, 1811.

JJ-III. DAVID JERVEY, b. Aug. 25, 1775, m. Feb. 26, 1806, SARAH CAPERS, dau. of Gabriel Capers. David was a physician. He d. 1851.

> *JJ-1. Thomas Hall, b. Jan., 1807, m. Jan. 3, 1833, Angelina Dorrill. He d. at Mt. Pleasant in 1872.
> *JJ-2. Gabriel Capers, m. Eliza Henrietta Capers, dau. of John Singeltary Capers. He was killed at First Manassas, 1863.
> JJ-3. James, m. Susan Sarah Evans and lived in Christ Church Parish, S. C. His will is dated June 16, 1853. They had (A) Maurice Simons, b. in 1850, (B) James David, b. in 1852, married and had issue, (C) Martha, d. in childhood and (D) Henrietta, d. age 16.
> JJ-4. Richard, m. and had a dau. Sallie who d. unm.
> JJ-5. Maurice Simons, m. Martha Fraser and d. without issue.
> JJ-6. Grace Hall, d. unm.
> JJ-7. Annie, d. unm.

JJ-1. THOMAS HALL JERVEY and ANGELINA DORRILL. *The Charleston Mercury,* Tuesday, Jany. 8, 1838 "On Thursday Morning last, by Rev. Dr. McDowall, Mr. Thomas Jervey of Christ Church Parish, to Miss Angeline youngest daughter of R. Dorrill, Esq. of this City."

> JJ-8. Sarah Martha, b. Jan. 14, 1834, d. y.
> JJ-9. Thomas Hines, d. y.
> JJ-10. Robert David, d. y.

JJ-11. Child, d. in inf.

JJ-12. Eliza Ann Alston, b. Sept., 1840, m. April, 1868, Dr. John Y. DuPré. She d. Feb. 24, 1900.

JJ-13. Mary Edwards, b. Dec., 1842, m. April, 1866, Thomas Choate.

JJ-14. Angelina Gabriella, b. Dec., 1844, m. 1862, the Rev. U. Sinclair Bird.

JJ-15. Pauline Henrietta.

JJ-16. Susan Jones, b. March, 1848, d. unm., Feb. 19, 1900.

JJ-17. Daniel DuPré, b. March, 1851, m. 1884, Katie Cherry.

JJ-18. Theodore Wagner, b. May, 1853, d. Jan. 21, 1859, Laurel Grove, Christ Church Parish.

JJ-19. Florence Evelyn, b. July, 1854, m. James Dooley.

JJ-20. John Leland, d. in inf.

JJ-2. GABRIEL CAPERS JERVEY m. ELIZA HENRIETTA CAPERS.

JJ-21. James Edward, lived Sumter, S. C.

JJ-22. William Capers, twin, to James Edward, killed in battle at Petersburg, Va.

JJ-23. Sarah Capers.

JJ-24. Annie Simons.

JJ-25. Sophia.

JJ-26. John Singeltary, 3rd Sgt., 23rd Reg't., S.C.V., when killed at Petersburg, Va., June 17, 1864.

JJ-27. Mary Capers.

JJ-28. Grace Hall.

JJ-29. Louis D.

JJ-30. Martha Jane.

JOHNSON FAMILY (Jo)

DR. WILLIAM HENRY JOHNSON, b. Mar. 30, 1871, m. May 5, 1898, LOTTIE PALMER CAPERS, b. Aug. 12, 1871, Greenville, S. C., dau. of Bishop Ellison Capers and Charlotte Rebecca Palmer. William Manigault Capers notes that she was the most loving and generous person who kept up with her family by one thoughtful deed after another. Dr. Johnson d. Apr. 14, 1934.

Dr. Johnson's book, "A Partial Genealogy of Wm. Johnson, III." has been a wonderful contribution to the genealogy of this family, as well as to many others.

Jo-1. James Reid, b. Apr. 12, 1899, graduate U. S. Naval Academy, June 1922, m. Dec. 30, 1922, Neva Fenno Palmer, dau. of George Smith Palmer and Neva Fenno, at New London, Ct. Issue: (A) Anne Palmer, b. Aug. 10, 1924, New London, m. William Ross Banks, Capt. U.S.N., (1972) and had (a) Ellison, (b) William Ross, Jr. and (c) Ann Broughton Banks. (B) Neva Palmer, b. Mar. 31, 1926, called "ChiChi", m. Roger B. Herrington and had (a) Ann Olivia, (b) Elizabeth and (c) Philip Herrington. (C) Diane Capers, b. Feb. 27, 1929, New London, m. George C. White and had (a) Shelly, (b) James, (c) Peter, (d) Neva and (e) Rebecca White. (D) Reida Johnson, m. Charles Kimmel and had one child.

Jo-2. Lottie Palmer Capers, b. May 27, 1903, m. June 2, 1924, Gerald Carthrae Thomas, Gen., U.S.M.C., (Ret.) son of O'Vander Wyatt Thomas, b. 1873, and Virginia Harrell Young, b. 1870. Gerald was b. Slater, Mo., Oct. 29, 1894. Issue: (A) Lottie Capers, b. Jan. 17, 1926, m. Joseph Andrew Bruder, April 14, 1951, Col., U.S.M.C. (Ret.). He was b. Apr. 22, 1918. They had (a) Anne Elizabeth, b. Apr. 2, 1952, Quantico, Va., (b) Charlotte Capers, b. Feb. 23, 1955, Paris, France, (c) Joseph Andrew, Jr., b. Sept. 15, 1956, Paris, France, (d) Catherine Palmer, b. Apr. 15, 1959, Camp Pendleton, Calif. and (e) Mary Caroline, b. Apr. 21, 1963, Portsmouth, Va.

(B) Gerald Carthrae, Jr., b. May 6, 1929, Col., U.S.M.C., m. Lydia Dean Dubblede, Aug. 14, 1954, who was b. Dec. 6, 1932. Issue: (a) Virginia Leigh, b. Jan. 7, 1956, Quantico, Va., (b) Susan Burnham, b. Sept. 13, 1957, Honolulu, Hawaii, and (c) Gerald Carthrae III, b. Aug. 26, 1962, Camp Pendleton, Calif.

(C) Virginia Young, b. Jan. 25, 1935, Fredericksburg, Va., m. John Richards Andrews, Jan. 9, 1955, who was b. Apr. 8, 1929, and had (a) Elizabeth Couturier, b. Dec. 4, 1955, Quantico, Va., (b)

Catherine Reed, b. Feb. 9, 1959, Washington, D. C., and (c) Thomas Richards Andrews, b. Nov. 21, 1968, Washington, D. C.

(D) William Henry Johnson Thomas, b. Mar. 17, 1937, Peiping, China. W. H. J. Thomas is a staff reporter with the CHARLESTON EVENING POST, Charleston, S. C. and is the author of the article "House is Undergoing Third Renovation" contained in this book. He has also been most helpful in furnishing information on this family.

Jo-3. Ellison Capers, b. June 3, 1907, Charleston, m. Margaret Eldredge Mikell, June 2, 1934. (Cmdr. U.S.N.R. Ret.) Issue: (A) Ellison Capers, Jr., b. May 27, 1937, Charleston, m. Rubydean Price and had (a) Heather Mikell, b. June 3, 1968 and (b) Anne Stuckey Johnson, b. July 24, 1970, (B) Beverly Mikell Johnson, b. Nov. 20, 1941, m. (1) Guerard Fuller Brown, Jr. and had (a) Virginia Gatewood Brown, b. Sept. 13, 1963 and (b) Guerard Fuller Brown III, b. Oct. 18, 1965. Beverly m. (2) Thomas John Riley and had (c) Thomas Patrick Riley, b. Mar. 28, 1971.

Jo-4. Mary Elizabeth, b. Oct. 2, 1910, m. Ernest Walter King, Jr., June 3, 1933, Grace Church, Charleston, S. C. He was son of Ernest W. King and Isabelle Ritchie Simmons of Hillsboro Plantation, St. Andrews Parish, Charleston Co., S. C. Issue: (A) Mary Elizabeth Johnson King, b. Nov. 13, 1935, m. John McNiel Hatcher, Major U.S.A., and had (a) John M. Hatcher, Jr., b. Jan. 5, 1962 and (b) Crispin King Hatcher, b. June 25, 1969.

JOHNSON LINE

I. WILLIAM JOHNSON I, arrived in Charleston, 1765, ae 24, Rep. of St. James Goose Creek in Legislature.

II. JAMES SLIDELL JOHNSON (8th son of above), m. ELEANOR SOPHIA REID, dau. of James Reid and Eleanor Gale Phillips.

III. WILLIAM JOHNSON III, b. 1821, Charleston, S. C. m. MARY HOLMES MELLICHAMP, on Apr. 4, 1861.

IV. WILLIAM HENRY JOHNSON, M.D., and CHARLOTTE PALMER CAPERS.

MELLICHAMP DESCENT

I. WILLIAM MELLICHAMP I, m. SARAH ST. LO who d. 1741.

II. THOMAS MELLICHAMP, d. Nov. 4, 1773, m. ELIZABETH ELLIOTT, dau. of Robert Elliott of Ashley River, S. C.

III. ST. LO MELLICHAMP, m. REBECCA STILES.

IV. THE REV. STILES MELLICHAMP (Prot. Epis. Ch.) m. SARAH FOWLER CROMWELL.

V. MARY HOLMES MELLICHAMP, b. Sept. 29, 1831, Gillisonville, S. C., d. Sept. 13, 1873, bur. Magnolia Cem., Chas.

Dr. William Henry Johnson, orthopedic surgeon and professor of orthopedics in the Medical College of the State of South Carolina, died yesterday afternoon at his home, 107 Wentworth street.

Funeral arrangements had not been completed last night, but it was announced by Connelley's that the service will be Monday afternoon.

Dr. Johnson, who was sixty-four years old on March 30, had served Charleston through a period of long, active and successful practice dating from 1900. He was a native of the city, a son of the late William Johnson and Mrs. Mary Holmes Mellichamp Johnson.

In 1898 Dr. Johnson was married to Miss Lottie Palmer Capers, daughter of Bishop Ellison Capers. Mrs. Johnson survives, with four children, Mrs. Gerald C. Thomas of Philadelphia; Mrs. Ernest W. King, Jr., and Ellison Capers Johnson, both of Charleston, and James Reid Johnson, 2nd, of New London, Conn.

Also surviving Dr. Johnson are two sisters, Mrs. Joseph S. Stevens, of Yonge's Island, and Mrs. John Frampton Maybank of Charleston, and a brother, James Reid Johnson, of Charleston.

Class of '91 at University

Spending his boyhood days in Charleston, Dr. Johnson attended private schools until he entered the University of South Carolina, where he completed a three-year scientific course in 1891. He entered the medical department of the University of Virginia, graduating in 1893.

Thereafter he received valuable training in several New York hospitals and pursued a brief course in the Bellevue Hospital Medical college. For two years he studied in clinics in Berlin.

Returning to Charleston Dr. Johnson entered into practice, but devoted much time to other activities. He taught in the Charleston Medical school, was connected with the Shirras Dispensary and for four years was city dispensary physician.

For several summers he taught at the University of the South and he also gave instruction in gynecology at the Charleston Polyclinic, and in roentology at the Medical college.

For nineteen months during the World war, a year of which was spent in France, Dr. Johnson was in active service. Dr. Johnson's war record as a surgeon was brilliant and he was several times recommended for promotion from the rank of captain, which he held. At one time, without other doctors, nurses or orderlies, Dr. Johnson had charge of 774 sick and wounded, who were in his care at the Mars sur Allier.

Lowcountry History Student

Dr. Johnson's career was not confined to medicine. He was regarded as an authority on the history and matters pertaining to the history of the Carolina Lowcountry. In this connection he had a vast collection of papers, manuscripts and other historical data.

His intense interest in matters pertaining to Lowcountry history took him into the field of genealogy. At the time of his death Dr. Johnson had nearly completed a volume on certain genealogies of Lowcountry families.

Dr. Johnson, an expert particularly in fracture work, was a surgical inventor, as well as practitioner. In the course of his practice he devised many ingenious splints used in the healing of difficult fractures.

Dr. Johnson was a member of the South Carolina Medical association, the American Medical association and other professional organizations. He was a member of the Phi Kappa Psi fraternity, of the St. Cecilia society and various social organizations. He had served as surgeon for the Carolina Rifles, as medical referee at the Charleston navy yard, physician to United States prisoners and as United States pension examiner. He was a member of Grace Protestant Episcopal church and for a score of years was a member of its vestry.

ANOTHER JOHNSON - CAPERS CONNECTION

SIR NATHANIEL JOHNSON, governor of S. C., 1702-1709, former governor of the Leeward Islands is a mutual ancestor of ELLISON CAPERS II and wife, CARLOTTA MANIGAULT BENBOW.

1. SIR NATHANIEL JOHNSON.	1. SIR NATHANIEL JOHNSON of "Silk Hope" plantation.
2. ANN JOHNSON m. GOVERNOR BROUGHTON who came to S. C. prior to 1696, trader, planter, soldier, d. ca. 1738.	2. ANN JOHNSON m. GOVERNOR BROUGHTON of "Mulberry" plantation.
3. CONSTANTIA BROUGHTON m. JOHN ASHLEY.	3. CHRISTIANNA BROUGHTON m. THE REV. (Episcopal) DANIEL DWIGHT in 1731, son of John Dwight of New Bedford, Mass.

4. ANN ASHLEY, in 1730 m. GABRIEL MANIGAULT, 1704-1781, son of Peter and Judith Manigault, emigrants to Carolina.

5. PETER MANIGAULT, 1731-1773, m. in 1755, ELIZABETH M. WRAGG, sister to Samuel Wragg who m. Judith Rothmahler and had a dau. Mary who m. Wm. Capers. She was dau. of Joseph Wragg and Judith DuBose, dau. of Jacques DuBose and Ann DuGué.

6. JOSEPH MANIGAULT, 1763-1843, m. 2ndly CHARLOTTE DRAYTON, dau. of Dr. Charles Drayton and Hester Middleton, 1781-1855, on May 27, 1800, at "Drayton Hall."

7. HENRY MIDDLETON MANIGAULT, 1811-1883, m. in 1837, SUSAN MIDDLETON LINING, dau. of Edward Blake Lining and Henrietta Parker.

8. CHARLOTTE DRAYTON MANIGAULT, m. as his second wife, WILLIAM WASHINGTON BENBOW, son of Martin and Sarah Agnew Humphreys Benbow; grandson of Adam Benbow and Susanna Green.

9. CARLOTTA MANIGAULT BENBOW, m. ELLISON CAPERS II.

4. SAMUEL DWIGHT, M.D., m. REBECCA MARION, niece of Gen. Francis Marion, dau. of Rebecca Allston, and Isaac Marion.

5. FRANCIS DWIGHT, who took Gen. Marion's name and his children were Marions instead of Dwight, he being the adopted son of Gen. Marion and his heir by will, married (1) CHARLOTTE KIRK in 1782 and in 1801, HARRIET KIRK, sisters and daus. of Gideon Kirk (son of Sarah D'Albiac and Wm. Kirk) and Rebecca Couturier, wid. of Peter Couturier.

6. CATHERINE MARION, b. Apr. 10, 1807 m. 1830, JOHN GENDRON PALMER, son of Elizabeth Catherine Porcher and Joseph Palmer.

7. CHARLOTTE REBECCA PALMER, m. 1859, ELLISON CAPERS I.

8. ELLISON CAPERS II, m. CARLOTTA MANIGAULT BENBOW.

MARION—PALMER FAMILY

1. Philip Gendron, to S. C. 1689   Benj. Marion, France to S. C. 1685
   Huguenot Leader   m. Judith Baluet, Huguenots

2. John Gendron   Gabriel Marion
                                    m. Esther Cordes

3. Marianne Gendron   Isaac Marion, Bro. of Swamp Fox
   m. John Palmer of Gravel Hill   m. Rebecca Alston

4. John Palmer of St. Stephens   Rebecca Marion
   m. Ann Cahusac   m. Samuel Dwight

5. Joseph Palmer of Springfield   Francis Marion (neé Dwight)
   m. Elizabeth Catherine Porcher   m. Charlotte Kirk
                                    m. Harriet Kirk

6. John Gendron Palmer of Cherry   Catherine Couturier Marion
   Grove m. Catherine Couturier   m. John Gendron Palmer
   Marion

7. Charlotte Rebecca Palmer   Charlotte Rebecca Palmer
   (1837-1908) m. Ellison Capers   m. Ellison Capers in 1859
   in 1859

The Harriet Marion Bible at The Citadel Library, Charleston, was a gift from her to her grand-daughter Charlotte Rebecca Palmer (Capers).

OWENS FAMILY (O)

CLARA STEWART CAPERS, dau. of Francis Withers Capers and Hannah Hawk Bascom, m. LAWRENCE BEACHAM OWENS, M.D. Issue:

*O-1. Frank Capers, M.D., m. Ida Rebecca Hand, of Columbia, S. C., dau. of Dr. William Harvey Hand and Edith Alice Gurley; granddau. of Moses Henry Hand and Mary Laura Ophelia Gaston.

O-2. Louise Beacham, 1901-1932, m. Joseph D. LaRoche. No issue.

O-1. FRANK CAPERS OWENS, M.D., mayor of Columbia, S. C. 1926-1941, Senator, WW II, Lt. Col. USAF, m. IDA REBECCA HAND.

O-3. Frances Rebecca, b. May 6, 1925, Columbia, m. Henry G. Turner, Jr. and had (A) Robert Henry, b. Feb. 22, 1946, m. Margaret Diane Miles in 1972, (B) Frances Rebecca, b. July 24, 1949 and (C) Frank Owens Turner, b. Aug. 22, 1950.

O-4. Vivian Capers, b. May 20, 1927, Columbia, m. Berkley Bryan Wilson, Dvd. Issue: (A) Vivian Capers, b. Nov. 15, 1952, (B) Berkley Bryan, Jr., b. April 17, 1955 and (C) Catherine Bryan Wilson, b. Jan. 20, 1959.

O-5. Louise Beacham, b. May 7, 1933, Columbia, m. Terrell L. Glenn and had (A) John Lyles, b. Nov. 8, 1956, (B) Terrell Lyles, Jr., b. May 6, 1958, (C) Rebecca Hand, b. May 17, 1964 and (D) Louise Owens Glenn, b. Jan. 15, 1969.

LAWRENCE BEACHAM OWENS, M.D. Though not a native of South Carolina, Dr. Owens is a member of an old and prominent family of this State and has spent the greater part of his life and his entire professional career as a physician and surgeon in South Carolina. Ever since the completion of his professional training Dr. Owens has practiced medicine and surgery at Columbia. He is not only one of the leading surgeons of South Carolina's capital, but for many years has been prominently active in public life and for the last five years has been mayor of Columbia. In this office he has given to the city a very efficient, honest and business-like administration and during his incumbency the record of the city has been one of steady progress. Of course, Dr. Owens is one of the best known and most popular citizens of Columbia, where his worth is fully recognized.

Lawrence Beacham Owens was born in Louisiana, February 25, 1860, a son of Dr. Stephen Lott and Sarah Marshall (Reese) Owens. His father was a native of Barnwell County, South Carolina, and a member of an old and prominent South Carolina family of English origin. The older Dr. Owens was graduated from the Medical College of South Carolina in 1858 and practiced medicine for some time in Barnwell County. At the outbreak of the War Between the States Dr. Stephen L. Owens became a surgeon with the Louisiana troops in the Confederate Army in Natchitoches Parish, from where he later moved to Bienville Parish. It was there that he died in 1875 and is buried in the Saline Baptist Church burying grounds. The grandfather of Dr. Lawrence B. Owens was Beacham B. Owens, who was a native and a prominent planter of Barnwell County. He married Nancy Taylor, a member of another old and prominent South Carolina family. The great-grandfather of Dr. Lawrence B. Owens was James Owens, a resident of South Carolina during the Revolutionary War period. Dr. and Mrs. Stephen L. Owens were the parents of four children, one of whom died young, those growing to maturity having been: 1. Ephraim S., now deceased. 2. Samuel H., a resident of Columbia. 3. Lawrence B., of whom further.

Dr. Owens received his early education in private schools and at the Oak Ridge Institute in North Carolina. Next he attended the University of South Carolina at Columbia, where he completed a two-year scientific course, graduating in pharmacy, and after that he took up the study of medicine at the Medical College of the State of South Carolina, from which he was graduated with the degree of Doctor of Medicine in 1893. After that he spent one year as an interne at Roper Hospital, Charleston. Having thus carefully prepared himself for his professional career, Dr. Owens came to Columbia and for a number of years engaged in general practice, later he specialized in the practice of surgery in South Carolina's capital. He enjoys a large and important practice, which, however, has not prevented him from taking a very active part in other phases of the community's life. In politics he is a staunch supporter of the Democratic party and for the last twenty-five years he has been one of his party's most active members and workers. In 1925 he was elected to the South Carolina Legislature from Richland County. In the following year, 1926, he was elected mayor of Columbia. He filled this office so capably and so entirely to the satisfaction of the entire community that, upon the expiration of his first term of four years, he was reelected mayor of Columbia in 1930 for a second term of four years. Dr. Owens is a man of progressive ideas and a keen supporter of aviation. Columbia's airport was named in honor of Dr. Owens and is popularly known as Owens Field. Dr. Owens is a member of the American Medical Association, the South Carolina State Medical Association, and the Columbia Medical Society, as well as of several other organizations, and is a member of the Baptist Church.

Dr. Owens married, April 16, 1895, Clara Stewart Capers, of Charleston, who died November 12, 1926. Mrs. Owens was a daughter of General Francis Withers Capers, of Georgia, and a niece of the late Bishop Ellison Capers of the Protestant Episcopal Church. Dr. and Mrs. Owens were the parents of two children: 1. Francis Capers Owens, M.D., now actively engaged in the practice of medicine at Columbia. He is a graduate of Columbia High School, the University of South Carolina and the School of Medicine of the University of South Carolina. He married Ida Hand, of Columbia, a daughter of Professor W. H. Hand, and they are the parents of two daughters, Frances Rebecca and Vivian Capers Owens. 2. Louise Beacham Owens, who married Joseph D. LaRoche, cashier of the Broad River Power Company at Columbia. She died in March, 1932. At that time the William Capers Chapter, Daughters of the American Revolution, passed the following resolutions:

WHEREAS, God in his infinite wisdom has seen fit to remove by death our friend and co-worker, Louise Owens LaRoche, and as she was doubly dear to this chapter because she was the daughter of Clara Capers Owens, a charter member of our chapter:

Be It Resolved, That we, the members of the William Capers Chapter, Daughters of the American Revolution, express our loss for this beautiful life so full of promise; that while we feel keenly the loss of one of our members who was so sincere in her unselfish service the memory of her life will always be cherished and that we extend our deepest love and heartfelt sympathy to her family and loved ones, and that a page in our minutes be dedicated to her memory, and that a copy of these resolutions be sent to her family and the press.

MRS. JAMES CATHCART,
MISS MATTYE P. IZARD,
MISS AGNES RICE MCMASTER.

History of South Carolina, Vol. IV, American Historical Society, 1935, Wallace, pp. 878-879.

SATTERLEE FAMILY (Sa)

CAPT. CHARLES BOOTHE SATTERLEE, USA, from Monroeton, Pa., graduate of high standing at West Point, m. MARY VIDEAU MARION CAPERS, dau. of Bishop Ellison Capers, Feb. 7, 1895, Trinity Church, Columbia, S. C. Capt. Satterlee died July 10, 1899, Honolulu, Hawaii.

Sa-1. John Franklin, b. Dec. 29, 1895, Columbia, S. C., m. June 8, 1927, at "Palmetto," Helen Laval DuPré, of McClellanville, S. C., dau. of John Young DuPré and Helen Louise Laval. John was veteran of W.W. I. They had (A) John Franklin II, b. May 31, 1928 and (B) Helen DuPré Satterlee, b. May 24, 1938, Columbia, S. C., m. April 15, 1961, Leonia, N. J., Kurt Theodore Speck, b. Oct. 3, 1934, Irvington, N. J., son of Kurt Speck and Lillian Mehle. Their issue: (A) Kurt Theodore, Jr., b. Jan. 17, 1962, (B) John Franklin Satterlee, b. Oct. 19, 1963, (C) William Henry Mehle, b. Apr. 10, 1967, and (D) Lillian DuPré Speck, b. Mar. 28, 1969. All issue born Englewood, N. J.

John F. Satterlee, Sr. d. Sept. 6, 1968, in Charleston, S. C. John F., Jr., d. Nov. 19, 1969, Clinton, S. C.

Sa-2. Charles Capers, D.D., Episcopal minister, now retired, b. Oct. 13, 1899, m. June 2, 1931, Frances Harrison Sparkman, b. Mar. 7, 1909, dau. of Frances Harrison of Atlanta, Ga. and Sullivan Thorne Sparkman of Dirleton Plantation, Pedee River (S. C.). Frances Sparkman was b. Columbia, S. C. Issue: (A) Frances Sparkman, b. Feb. 18, 1933, Columbia, m. Nov. 22, 1958, Mason Gardner Alexander, b. Sept. 11, 1932, Greenville, S. C., son of James Mason Alexander and Margaret Gardner and had (a) Mason G., Jr., b. Nov. 25, 1959, Spartanburg, S. C. and (b) dau. Ellison Capers Alexander, b. Aug. 7, 1961, Greenville, S. C., (B) Mary Capers, b. June 22, 1935, Birmingham, Ala., m. Aug. 21, 1958, Spartanburg, the Rev. Charles Adair Bledsoe, b. July 23, 1933, Perry, Ga., son of Daniel Webster Bledsoe and Lillian Adair. Issue: (a) Mary Capers, b. Sept. 20, 1959, Spartanburg, (b) Charles Adair, Jr., b. Apr. 9, 1962 and (c) Thorne Sparkman Bledsoe, b. Oct. 1, 1963, Rock Hill, S. C., (C) dau. Thorne Sparkman Satterlee, b. Oct. 15, 1937, Birmingham, Ala., m. June 15, 1963, Spartanburg, Paul Vernon Martin, Jr., b. Apr. 13, 1928, Greer, S. C., son of Paul Vernon Martin and Maybelle Davidson, and had (a) Frances Harrison, b. Aug. 21, 1969 and (b) Capers Satterlee Martin, b. Jan. 15, 1971, Spartanburg, S. C.

STEVENS FAMILY (S)

MARY SINGELTARY CAPERS m. in 1855, PETER FAYSSOUX STEVENS, professor at S. C. Military Academy, Col. C.S.A., and later Bishop of Reformed Protestant Episcopal Church. Bishop Stevens m. (2) HARRIET PALMER, dau. of Dr. Saunders Palmer, of "Ballsdam," and wife, Esther Simons. No issue this marriage.

Bishop Stevens was the son of Clement W. Stevens who m. in 1820, Sarah Johnston Fayssoux, b. 1795, dau. of Dr. Peter Fayssoux who m. 2ndly Mrs. Ann (Smith) Johnston, dau. of William Smith, in 1777.

ISSUE OF BISHOP STEVENS and MARY CAPERS.

S-1. Helen Capers, Feb. 19, 1859-Feb. 3, 1937, m. Daniel Allston DuPré, May 5, 1848-Sept. 6, 1930, professor of Wofford College, Spartanburg, S. C. He was son of Warren DuPré, b. 1816, professor at Wofford College many years, who m. as his second wife, May Ann Sydnor, 1822-1896, dau. of Lucy and Beverly Sydnor, of Boydton, Va. Warren DuPré was son of Daniel, b. St. James Santee, 1793, who m. in 1815, Sarah Margaret Hibben. Issue: (A) Fayssoux Stevens, (B) Mary Sydnor, (C) Helen Allston, (D) Grace Annette DuPré, a well-known artist.

S-2. The Rev. William, minister Reformed Episcopal Church m. Mattie Latane and had (A) Paul Stevens and others.

S-3. Dolores DelGardo, m. Edwin Cameron Holt, son of Laura Moore and James Holt, of N. C. and had Dolores Stevens Holt who m. ———— Cheatham, and had issue.

STONE FAMILY (St)

THE REV. GEORGE WASHINGTON WHITFIELD STONE, b. Nov. 28, 1818, in Columbia County, Ga., m. SUSAN BETHIA CAPERS, July 23, 1843. He died Aug. 30, 1889, Oxford, Ga. and is buried there. Dr. Stone graduated at Emory College in 1842 and was a member of the faculty, serving with only brief interruptions until shortly before his death. An officer of Emory at Oxford, Ga. he was more than once a secret benefactor of the college.

St-1. Susan Capers, b. Apr. 12, 1851, m. Jan. 21, 1892, W. F. Robison, and died July 15, 1925. Bur. Oxford, Ga. No issue.

St-2. Emma Sidney, b. July 31, 1853, m. Dec. 6, 1877, Howard E. W. Palmer, and d. Sept. 24, 1920. Bur. Atlanta, Ga. No issue.

St-3. George W. W. II, b. Dec. 18, 1855, d. Nov. 9, 1939, n. m. Bur. Oxford, Ga.

St-4. Sara Amanda, b. June 8, 1858, m. July 1, 1886, J. W. Branham, d. June 13, 1931, bur. Oxford, Ga. Issue: (A) Sara Elizabeth, b. July 25, 1888, m. Dec. 22, 1945, Philip S. Matthews, and d. Nov. 16, 1962. No issue. (B) George Harlan Branham, b. Apr. 6, 1892, d. Oct. 1, 1914, n. m.

*St-5. Harry Harlan, b. Nov. 18, 1861, m. July 15, 1885, Susan J. Bonnell, and d. Aug. 18, 1932. Bur. Oxford, Ga.

*St-6. William Theodotus, b. Dec. 25, 1864, m. Dec. 21, 1893, Ida Florence Lowrey, and d. Feb. 19, 1904. Bur. Oxford, Ga.

St-5. HARRY HARLAN STONE, born, married, and died Oxford, Ga. m. SUSAN J. BONNELL, b. Dec. 24, 1864, Macon, Ga., d. March 2, 1946, Oxford, Ga., dau. of the Rev. John Mitchell Bonnell and Mary Ann Eliza Morton. All issue born Oxford, Ga.

St-7. Margaret Judith, b. Apr. 29, 1886, d. May, 1887.

St-8. Bonnell Harold, b. Dec. 3, 1887, d. May 24, 1935, m. Dec. 28, 1912, Edna Ausland.

St-9. George Howard, b. Mar. 21, 1889, d. Oct. 24, 1941, n. m.

St-10. William Morton, b. Jan. 9, 1894, d. Oct. 21, 1902.

St-11. Emmalise Palmer, b. Apr. 21, 1897, living 1973. Miss Emmalise Stone kindly furnished all the material on the Stone family.

St-12. Susanne Elizabeth, b. Dec. 19, 1908, m. Dec. 19, 1933, Dr. Virgil Y. C. Eady, 1898-1969, Dean of Emory College, 1945-1966. He is bur. Oxford, Ga. Issue: Virgil Y. C., Jr.

St-6. WILLIAM THEODOTUS STONE m. IDA FLORENCE LOW-
REY.

St-13. William Lowrey, b. Oct. 7, 1894, m. Dec. 25, 1921, Una
Haddock, and d. Apr. 20, 1968. Bur. Blakely, Ga. Issue: (A)
Lowrey Standifer, b. Blakely, Ga., m. Ann Sims, Blakely, Ga.

*St-14. Harry Ryals, b. Oct. 7, 1896, m. Sept. 29, 1920, Alma May
Gunter, and d. Mar. 17, 1965. Bur. Oxford, Ga. He was a tele-
phone executive with Southern Bell in Atlanta, Ga.

St-15. Son, b. ca. 1898, Macon Ga. d. inf., bur. Oxford, Ga.

St-16. Florence Ida (called Polly), b. Feb. 26, 1901, m. Aug. 1,
1934, Norman Sydney Buck: Issue: (A) Caroline, b. May 18,
1935, New Haven, Conn., d. of leukemia, Jan. 15, 1950, New
Haven, bur. Wilmington, Mass. where all her Buck relatives are
bur. since first coming to this country in the early part of 17th
century, (B) Judith, b. New Haven, Apr. 27, 1938, M.A. degree,
Yale U., 1960, m. David Stuart Moore, Aug. 4, ———, Dwight
chapel, Yale, and had (a) Sydney Nettleton (called Steve), b.
New Haven, 1964 and (b) Peter Stuart Moore, b. New Haven,
1967, (C) Alison Buck, b. New Haven, June 4, 1939, grad. Mt.
Holyoke College, 1961, m. James Scott Cook, chapel of North-
field School, Sept. 13, 1970.

St-17. Elizabeth, b. Oct. 4, 1904, d. Feb. 1905, bur. Oxford, Ga.

St-14. HARRY RYALS STONE, m. ALMA MAY GUNTER.

St-18. Elizabeth (called Betsy), b. New York City, m. (1) Lamar
Pierson, in Atlanta, Ga., dvd. but had two daus., (A) Betty Lou,
who m. Robert Hudsco Yevich, and (B) Margy Pierson. She m.
(2) Dr. ———.

St-19. Harry Harlan, M.D., Phi Beta Kappa, Yale U., grad. Johns
Hopkins and Emory U., m. Jean Martin, Atlanta. Issue: (A)
Sandy, (B) Bill and (C) Clay.

ZEMP FAMILY (Z)

DR. FRANCIS LESLIE ZEMP, 1819-1893, was brought to this country from Switzerland in 1825 by his father, who died of yellow fever the same year in Charleston. Apparently having no relatives he was placed in the Charleston Orphan Asylum. He later moved to Camden, S. C. where he worked and studied in Dr. Joshua Reynolds' drug store. He married Rebecca, dau. of Dr. Reynolds and had a dau., SOPHIA, 1844-1918, who m. at age 18, SAMUEL ELIZABETH CAPERS (C-57). Dr. Zemp m. (2) ABATHIAH ELIZABETH CAPERS, dau. of Samuel Wragg Capers and wife, Abathiah Harvey Thornton.

Dr. Zemp graduated from the U. of Pa., qualifying as a physician and a pharmacist, first practicing in Sumter then Camden and became one of the town's most successful doctors and business men.

Z-1. Francis Leslie, 1850-1915, m. Emma Hamlin.

Z-2. William Harvey, 1852-1912, m. Alice Brunson.

*Z-3. Eugene Capers, 1854-1903, m. Mary Grizella Blakeney.

Z-4. Mary Adella, 1858-1920, m. N. B. Rankin.

Z-5. Jessie Lee, 1862-1893, m. (1) John Arthur and (2) L. Means.

Z-6. Charles Herbert, d. y.

Z-7. Elizabeth Capers, d. y.

Z-8. Francis M., 1860——— m. (1) Kate DeLoache and (2) Nadine Dabney.

Z-9. Sidney Capers, b. 1868, m. (1) Hattie Truesdale and (2) Gertrude Mitcham.

Z-10. Ernest Russell, b. 1871, grad. S. C. Military Academy, 1890, later obtained M.D. from College of Physicians and Surgeons, m. Kathleen Hunt, of Ala.

Z-11. Annie Braxton, b. 1867, m. Dr. W. S. Stokes.

Z-3. EUGENE CAPERS ZEMP, b. Oct. 17, 1854, d. Nov. 16, 1903, m. MARY GRIZELLA BLAKENEY, dau. of Virginia DuBose (dau. of Isaiah DuBose and Gilly Hinton Benton) and General James White Blakeney. Mary was b. Apr. 21, 1850, d. Dec. 4, 1916.

Z-12. Louise Blakeney, b. Aug. 17, 1877, m. William R. DeLoache and had (A) Eugene Capers, b. Aug. 14, 1904, (B) Elizabeth Palmer, b. June 18, 1906, (C) Virginia Blakeney, b. Oct. 8, 1910, (D) Charles Herbert, b. July 1, 1913, (E) Ruth Redding, b. Feb. 17, 1915 and (F) William Redding DeLoache, b. Mar. 17, 1920.

*Z-13. Charles Herbert, b. Sept. 8, 1879, d. 1901, m. Nov. 4, 1900, Mary K. Shannon.

Z-14. Henrietta DuBose, b. June 26, 1881, d. 1969.

Z-15. Albert Sidney, b. Mar. 15, 1883, m. June 1, 1913, Irma Hubert and had (A) Albert Sidney, Jr., b. Aug. 20, 1914 and (B) William Pahl, b. Nov. 17, 1915.

Z-16. Elizabeth Capers, b. Aug. 20, 1884, m. the Rev. Palmer Clisby DuBose.

Z-17. James Blakeney, b. Nov. 11, 1886, m. Oct. 16, 1912, Bertie Moore Lenoir.

Z-18. Ernest Capers, b. July 18, 1889, m. Dec. 28, 1914, Dora Amanda Roof, and d. June 20, 1961. They had (A) Barbara Ann, b. Mar. 25, 1918, Camden, S. C., m. Roderick Hill Cantey, Aug. 9, 1941, a son of Harry Cantey and Mary Wood Hill and had (a) Barbara Zemp, b. July 20, 1942, (b) Roderick Hill, Jr., b. Dec. 22, 1944, (c) Mary Hill, b. Oct. 11, 1946, (d) Claudia Henderson Cantey, b. Aug. 30, 1948. All born in Camden, S. C. (B) Mary Blakeney Zemp, b. Aug. 18, 1920.

Z-19. Benton Cassels, b. May 6, 1892.

Z-13. CHARLES HERBERT ZEMP, 1879-1901, m. MARY K. SHANNON.

Z-20. Charles Herbert, Jr., b. Oct. 23, 1901, Camden, S. C., m. Sept. 22, 1926, Camden, Elizabeth Brisbane Workman, b. June 18, 1903, dau. of John James Workman (son of W. H. R. Workman and Keturah Gatewood) and Martha Rives Boykin (dau. of Samuel Francis Boykin and Margaret Douglas Ancrum). Issue: (A) Charles Herbert, b. June 11, 1927, Charlotte, N. C., m. (1) Virginia Selden Rhett, July 19, 1948, in Charleston, S. C., dau. of Robert Barnwell Rhett and Virginia Prettyman. He m. (2) Genevieve Harden. No issue second marriage. By first marriage: (a) Virginia Rhett, b. Feb. 2, 1949, Charleston, (b) Elizabeth Workman, b. Jan. 13, 1950, Charleston, (c) Charles Herbert, b. Sept. 10, 1952, Charleston, (d) Barnwell Rhett, b. Mar. 3, 1955, Camden, S. C., d. Sept. 17, 1971, (e) Mary Shannon, b. Sept. 30, 1956, Camden and (f) Douglas Boykin, b. Jan. 21, 1958, Camden. (B) John Workman, b. Sept. 28, 1931, Camden, m. Dec. 20, 1958, Lois Virginia DeWitt, in Columbus, Ohio. She was b. Oct. 10, 1930, Columbus, dau. of Louis Napoleon DeWitt II and Louisa Virginia Boggess. They had (a) John Workman, b. Mar. 13, 1960, Chelsea, Mass., (b) Virginia DeWitt, b. June 17,

1961, Chelsea, (c) James Blakeney, b. Oct. 10, 1962, Chelsea and (d) Louis DeWitt, b. Sept. 1, 1966, Chapel Hill, N. C. (C) Francis Lachicotte, b. July 24, 1937, Camden, m. Dec. 22, 1959, Phyllis Carrison Wooten, dau. of Francis McNair Wooten and Phyllis Carrison, and had (a) Francis Lachicotte, b. Sept. 1, 1960, (b) James Lenoir Haile, b. Feb. 19, 1965.

MARY KERSHAW SHANNON was dau. of Mary Kershaw and Charles John Shannon; granddau. of Joseph B. Kershaw and Lucretia Douglas; great-granddau. of Harriet DuBose and Col. John Kershaw; gr-gr-granddau. of Isaac DuBose IV and Catherine DuTarque and of Joseph Kershaw, b. ca. 1728, Yorkshire, England, who came to S. C. ca. 1750, and married Sarah Mathis, ca. 1763.

EARLY RECORDS OF RICHARD CAPERS I OR SEA ISLAND LINE

Know all men by these presents that RICHARD CAPERS and RICHARD RENOLDS—are held and firmly Bound unto ye honourable Coll Robt Gibbs Esqr: Governour SC in ye Just and full Sum of Two Thousand pound Sterlin—Twenty second day of February Anno Dom 1710—The Condition of this obligation is such y^t ye above Bounden Richard Capers—is appoynted Guardion and Tutor of ye persons and portion of Thomas Capers . . . Being in his minority if therefore he ye said Richard Capers . . . shall well and truly bring up ye said Thomas Capers . . . with convenient meat drinke apparell & Education dureing his minority and dureing ye time he shall be Guardian and Tutor unto ye said Thomas Capers . . . and shall dureing that time Defend him from hurt of Body loss of Goods or Lands in any wise so far forth as his . . . power Lieth and such portin as shall fall Due by ye Death and Inventory of ye said deceased: shall Truly pay unto ye said Thomas Capers . . . within three months next after shall accomplish ye Age of Twenty one yeares . . . and if he dy before Such time then to his Executors, Administrators or to Such other person or persons as ye Law shall Limitt and apoynt & further shall make.

RICH^D CAPERS (Seal)

RICH^D RENOLDS. R. Marke (Seal)

DAVID ADAMS & ELIZABETH his wife, "one of the Daughters of Richard Capers of this Province Plant^r. Deceased, Doe hereby Acknowledge to have Reced of Mr William Chapman of the Same Province Tanner and Mary his wife Admors to the Estate of Said Richd Capers Deced the full and Just Sum of Twenty five Pounds Sterling money of this Part of this Province . . . Feb. 20, 1710-11

RICHARD CAPERS Lawfull Guardian unto THOMAS CAPERS Son of Richd Capers of this Province Planter. Deced doe hereby acknowledge to have Received (for the use of the Said Thomas Capers) of Mr. William Chapman of this Said Provence—the full and Just Sum of Twenty five pounds Sterling curr^t money of this Part of the Province . . . Feb. 20, 1710-11

Will of WILLIAM CAPERS of St. Helena, dated May 22, 1827, proved
Sept. 6, 1827.

Mentions: late uncle, John E. Farr
        friend, Daniel Ravenel, and brother Thomas F. Capers,
        execs.
        brother, Dr. Charles W. Capers, of St. Helena.

". . . Diamond buckel one of a pair bequeathed to me by my
uncle Thomas Bradford Smith—be set as a necklace and that a pair of
Diamond Earrings and a finger ring be purchased with a part of the
aforesaid five hundred Dollars to match the aforesaid necklace and
that the remaining part or portion of the said five hundred Dollars be
left in trust to my said Brother Thomas F(arr?) Capers be applied to
the purchase of a Ladies Gold Watch, Chain & Seal & 'c elegant and
ornamental, all of which I give & bequeath to my beloved cousin Amelia
Martha Bulkley, Daughter of John Bulkley, merchant of New York,
as a small testimony of the sincere affection which I entertained for her
to the moment of my death.

. . ."wish and request that my body be opened by my friend Dr.
Thomas Y. Simons for examination in order to benefit medical science,
then be placed in a plain cedar coffin & deposited in the family vault
at Hickory Hill, St. Andrews Parish & District . . . along side my uncle
John E. Farr, and that my funeral be attended only by immediate
friends and relatives and that no particular form or funeral ceremony
be used by any particular minister but simply a prayer to Almighty
God of his infinite mercy to receive my Soul, be offered by a minister
of any denomination whatever . . ."

EARLY RECORDS OF RICHARD CAPERS LINE

Stub Entries to Indents Issued in Payment of Claims Against South
Carolina Growing Out of the Revolution.

No. 91   Issued to Mr Charles Capers for Forty Nine pounds thirteen
Book D   Shillings and Eleven Pence Sterling for One Cask Indico
Page 149   weight Nett two hundred and forty two pounds, impressed
        from him by Order of Governor Rutledge in January 1782
        Acount Audited, 20th decemb. 1783

        Principal £49..13..11   Interest £3..9..6

No. 91   Issued the 20th december 1783 to Mr. Charles Capers for
Book D   twenty three pounds Eleven Shillings and 4d Sterling for

Page 163   Provisions supplied the Continental Army
Account Audited

Principal £23..11..4   Interest £1..12..11

MISCELLANEOUS RECORDS OF RICHARD CAPERS LINE

1820 *Census, South Carolina, Beaufort County* lists:
Dr. Charles W. Capers and Charles G(abriel?) Capers.
(I found none listed for Charleston County, Christ Church Parish.)

1860 *Census, Beaufort* lists: (St. Helena Parish)
F. T. CAPERS, age 30, planter, value of real estate $13,500.

W. G. CAPERS, age 30, planter, wife, ARABELLA, age 20, married within the year. 1870 *Census* for town of Beaufort, lists WILLIAM G. CAPERS, age 39, ISABELLA, age 28 and William 9/12 (9 months old).

EDW. M., age 42, planter.

C. B., age 52, planter, b. in S. C., wife, MARY, age 43, Benjamin, age 7, Elirth, female, age 5, and Edward, age 2.

1850 *Census for St. Helena Parish, Beaufort County, S. C.* lists:
C. G. CAPERS, age 75, planter; MARY, age 50; Benj., 35; Edw., 30; Ann E. Mynott, 25; Fra^s T., 22; Wm. G., 18; Thomas, 16.

DIRECT TAX BEAUFORT (S. C.) CASES
PETITIONS, BRIEFS, RECORDS, VOL. I.

1892. EDWARD M. CAPERS v. U. S.
Place on St. Helena called Edward Capers Place, 165 acres, and ½ part of island called Capers' Island, 150 acres. Sold under U. S. Direct Tax Acts March 1863.

MARCH 1863, ST. HELENA PARISH

W. Perry Capers, Mary E. Phillips, James F. DeBow Capers, Charles S. G. Capers, Arabella A. Capers v. U. S. Gabriel Capers' Place and Capers Island.

W. Gabriel Capers died 1882, intestate, and claimants are his heirs-at-law. Also place known as the "Perry Place" said Sarah H. Perry d. 1867, claimants as her heirs-at-law.

DR. FRANCIS T. CAPERS, b. 1830, St. Helena Island, physician (1892) went to school with Dr. W. J. Jenkins, had known him all his life. Dr. Capers married Miss Bourkin. Large slave owner (over 100) at "Half-way House" plantation, St. Helena Parish, Beaufort Dist.

RICHARD CAPERS I LINE (Rc)

RICHARD I, m. MARY BARNETT, probably sister of William Barnett of Jamaica Island. Richard was a cordwainer. After his death his wid., Mary, m. William Chapman.

"CHARLESTON COUNTY, S. C.
Mar: 10, 1694/5
    This day Mrs Mary Capers, widdow & Relictt of Mr Richard Capers late of this P^rvince Deceased: came and Entered a Caviatt to the Estate of her said Deceased Husband as aforesaid, & prays Letters of Administration uppon the goods & Chattles, Rights and Creditts of her said Husbands Estate . . ."

"COURT OF ORDINARY, Oct. 28, 1695.
    "William Chapman etc. made an inventory & appraisement of the goods of Richard Capers shown to them by Mrs. Mary Capers, wid. March 15, 1694/5. They executed their bond to Gov. Blake for Mrs. Capers faithful execution of her trust. Gov. Blake directed Mrs. Capers to administer the estate of Richard Capers, deceased, and directed William Chapman and others to make an inventory of the estate."

WILLIAM CHAPMAN'S will, probated April 1, 1711, Charles Town, tanner, asks to be bur. James Island. Mentions: son, William, 17, unm.; Richard and Thomas, sons of Richard Capers; Mary, wife of Richard Reynolds; Elizabeth, wife of David Adams; Thomas, son of Richard Capers, dec.

SUSANNA GRIFFIN, wid. of Benjamin, late of Charles City, mariner, in her will dated Mar. 4, 1722, probated Jan. 10, 1728, (must have been a sister of Mary Barnett) mentions nephews Richard Capers, Thomas Capers, of Charles City, joiner, and several Barnett nephews. She mentions among others nieces: Elizabeth Adams, wid. of David Adams, mariner; and Mary Reynolds, wife of Richard Reynolds, cordwainer.

    Rc-1. Elizabeth, m. (1) David Adams, mariner and (2) John Jenkins, I.

*Rc-2. Richard, II, bur. Oct. 20, 1754, age 74, m. Rebecca ————.
    First settled on Stono then St. Helena's Island.

    Rc-3. Charles. He and his brother Thomas are perhaps the ones on the List of the Two Companys on Port Royal and St. Helens (sic)

Island Port Royal Company. (Muster Rolls of the S. C. Granville and Colleton County Regiments of Militia, 1756.

Rc-4. Mary, m. Richard Reynolds.

*Rc-5. Thomas of Edisto, m. Mary Sadler.

Rc-2. RICHARD CAPERS, 2 (Richard 1), m. REBECCA ————, who must have predeceased him for his will, dated 1741, proved March 3, 1755 does not mention her. He, then of St. Helena Island, Granville, asks that his body be decently interred in a Christian like manner in the church yard at Bealefast (?). He mentions Mary Adams (Nathaniel), dau. Ann Morgan, sons, Joseph and William Capers. Nathaniel Adams was named as executor. His will also mentions

. . . his island known as Coopers Island to go to dau. Ann Morgan

. . . land at Combahee (500 acres)

. . . land where he resides, St. Helena (250 acres) and where he lives with daughter, Mary Adams

. . . land next to William Chapman "whereon my tanning vats are made"

. . . 1500 acres of land upon an Island which is known by the name of Capers Hunting Island to go to son Joseph and dau. Mary Adams

. . . "all my Negroes men women or children, Indians and slaves to be sold after this crop is cleaned and the money to be divided."

Rc-6. Anne, m. Joshua Morgan of London, bachelor, in 1740 (St. Helena Rec.) They had (A) Anne, b. Feb. 17, 1741 and (B) Susannah, b. July 13, 1742 who m. April 28, 1763, ———— Capers. Joshua m. (2) Magdalen Albergotti, spinster.

*Rc-7. Joseph Ellicott, m. Dec. 21, 1740, Hannah Adams Frampton, wid. He was bur. Dec. 4, 1743 and she m. (3) Middleton Evans.

Rc-8. Mary, m. Aug. 14, 1740, Nathaniel Adams.

Rc-9. William.

Rc-10. Susan, bur. Oct. 16, 1740.

Rc-5. THOMAS CAPERS, 2 (Richard 1), m. MARY SADLER. His will is dated 1761 of Charles Town. He was among the sufferers in the Charleston fire of 1740. The S. C. Gazette advertized Nov. 7, 1741 that each sufferer was directed to submit a schedule of loss, the committee would study the same and apportion the sum to be granted each person. Thomas Capers was granted 71 pounds sterling, which in most cases was about one-third the amount of the loss.

Rc-11. Charles, m. Nov. 13, 1755, Anne Thomson, spinster, b. Aug. 13, 1737, dau. of Francis and Constantia Thomson. They had (A) Elizabeth who m. Feb. 24, 1785, Thomas Ladson, son of Benjamin and Elizabeth Ladson of St. Helena. He was bp. June 27, 1756, (B) Ann, b. Nov. 23, 1770, (C) Constance, b. Aug. 15, 1756. (From St. Helena Parish Records.)

Rc-12. Richard, of Hilton Head, m. Nov. 29, 1767, Elizabeth Rachel Spencer, spinster, by the Rev. Robert Smith. They had (A) Charles, bp. Jan. 7, 1785 who m. Mar. 12, 1808, Mary Capers, (B) Joseph, b. Aug. 18, 1770.

Rc-13. Thomas, m. Elizabeth Guy, spinster, Dec. 8, 1767, by the Rev. Robert Smith. (St. Philips Parish Reg.)

Rc-14. Elizabeth, m. Edmund Ellis, bachelor, son of Edmund, bur. 1734, and Anne, bur. 1738. Edmund, Jr. was b. Aug. 26, 1724.

Rc-15. Ann m. ———— Bollard.

Rc-16. Mary, bp. June 8, 1729.

Rc-7. JOSEPH ELLICOTT CAPERS, 2 (Richard 1), m. HANNAH ADAMS FRAMPTON, wid. His will, dated Nov. 29, 1743, says he is a planter of St. Helena Island, Granville Co., S. C. Mentions his wife and two sons and "brother" Nathaniel Adams. Proved April 5, 1744.

Rc-17. Richard, b. Nov. 23, 1741, d. Nov. 25, 1741, St. Helena Rec.

Rc-18. William, b. Sept. 18, 1743, d. Aug. 16, 1745, St. Helena Rec.

ADAMS FAMILY (A)

ELIZABETH CAPERS, dau. of Richard Capers I and Mary Barnett, m. (1) DAVID ADAMS, mariner from New England, b. 1682, d. ca. 1720. Elizabeth m. (2) JOHN JENKINS, SR.

*A-1. David, Jr., ca. 1718-ca. 1786, m. (1) Ann Jenkins, Dec. 6, 1739, dau. of John Jenkins, Sr., his step-father; m. (2) Feb. 1, 1753, Catherine Grimball, b. ca. 1737, spinster, dau. of Paul and Mary Grimball.

A-2. Mary, b. ca. 1712, m. (1) May 23, 1727, John Jenkins, Jr., b. ca. 1706, she being step-daughter to his father. John d. 1756, intestate and she m. (2) William Mason of Charleston, before Feb. 7, 1759 and lived in Charleston.

A-3. Hannah, m. (1) in 1731, John Frampton; (2) in 1750 her cousin Joseph Ellicott Capers and (3) at St. Helena, Middleton Evans, bachelor from James Island. (St. Helena Rec.)

A-4. Nathaniel, bachelor of St. Helena m. (1) Aug. 14, 1740, Mary Capers, spinster, and (2) Sept. 6, 1744, Margaret Ellis, dau. of Edmund and Anne Ellis, and sister to Edmund Ellis who m. Elizabeth Capers (Rc-14). Issue: by second wife. (A) David, b. Sept. 2, 1745, (B) Nathaniel, Jr., b. Dec. 20, 1747, (C) Edmund, b. Dec. 27, 1749 and (D) —————, b. July 2, 1752.

A-1. DAVID ADAMS, JR. m. and had issue one being

A-5. David, who m. (1) Ann Chaplin and (2) Mary Laurence. In *The Bells and Allied Families* by Maria Lock Bell, 1953, she traces their child BENJAMIN ADAMS who m. MARY REBECCA CHAPLIN to MARY CHAPLIN ADAMS who m. THEODORE AUGUSTUS BELL and they had JOHN BELL who m. EMILY MARGARET MILLIGAN.

Helen Iredell Jones, b. Rock Hill, Dec. 30, 1878, d. June 13, 1966, Columbia, S. C., m. in Columbia, June 14, 1900, Joseph Milligan Bell, b. Sept. 15, 1876, d. Columbia, S. C., March 3, 1958, son of John Bell of Beaufort, S. C. and Emily Margaret Milligan of Augusta, Ga. Their issue: (A) Joseph Milligan, Jr., b. Columbia, June 17, 1903, m. in New York, Sept. 15, 1933, Evangeline Bell, b. Dec. 25, 1904, dau. of Arthur F. Bell, of Charlottetown, Prince Edward Island, and Sarah MacKenzie. They had (a) Evangeline Iredell, b. New York, April 11, 1936, m. in Paris, France, Nov. 21, 1964, Jordan Kirsch, (b) twins, Judith Milligan, b. N. Y. April 11, 1936, m. Jan. 20, 1962 at Binghamton, N. Y., David Nelson Boucher, b. Oct. 12, 1935, son of Robert Vaughn

Boucher and Ruth Burrows Baker of State College, Pa. They had David
Nelson Boucher, Jr., b. Jan. 29, 1963, (B) John Bell, b. Columbia, S. C.,
July 10, 1906, m. in Orangeburg, S. C., Oct. 15, 1936, Henrietta Estelle
Brantley, b. Orangeburg, S. C., July 11, 1909, dau. of Thomas Frederick
Brantley and Estelle Fairey. They had: (a) John, Jr., b. Feb. 2, 1940,
m. Jan. 25, 1964, Virginia Joan Davis, b. Mar. 25, 1940, Charleston,
S. C., dau. of Herbert C. Davis and Doris Virginia Glaus, and had (1)
John Davis, b. Sept. 2, 1966, Portsmouth, R. I. and (2) Helen Virginia
Davis Bell, b. Columbia, S. C., Sept. 9, 1969, (b) Henrietta Brantley,
b. Apr. 22, 1944, m. the Rev. George Kenneth Grant Henry, b. Charlotte,
N. C., Oct. 21, 1942, and had (1) Elizabeth Brantley, b. Alexandria, Va.,
Sept. 28, 1969, (2) Mary Ellison Henry, b. Aug. 27, 1971, Athens, Ga.
The Rev. George Henry is the son of the Rt. Rev. and Mrs. M. St.
George Henry, Bishop of Western North Carolina, Episcopal Church.
(C) Helen Iredell born Columbia, S. C., Dec. 15, 1909, d. March 2,
1971 in Columbia, n. m.

NOTE:

A-4. (B) "Nathanial Adams, Esq. of White Bluff, Ga., second son of
Nathanial Adams of St. Helena, S. C. was born Dec. 20, 1747, on
St. Helena Island, S. C. He went to Georgia and was a planter,
owning the old Adams place at White Bluff near Savannah, a gentleman of the 'Old School', a Tory, preferring to adhere to the Crown,
and dying in 1806, after holding the position of Justice of the Peace,
a position of honor." * He married Anne Bolton, dau. of Robert
Bolton of Savannah, 1722-1789, and Susannah Mauvé, 1727-1762.
Robert Bolton held many public positions in Savannah, and was
the first Postmaster in Georgia.

Nathanial Adams and Anne Bolton had (A) Nathaniel who m.
Mary Ann Wylly and (B) Susan Ann who m. Dec. 11, 1809, John
Lewis, Esq., 1785-1867. Their dau. (a) Ann Margaret Lewis m.
Noble Andrew Hardee of Savannah, 1805-1867, in 1835, son of John
Hardee, 1775-1839, and Sarah, dau. of Thomas Ellis.

Noble Andrew Hardee and Ann Margaret Lewis had a son,
John Lewis Hardee, b. 1836, who m. in 1861, Mary Helen Stoddard,
dau. of John Stoddard, and had Marie Eliza Hardee who m. Clifford
Alonzo King, youngest son of Barrington King and Catherine Martha
Esther Nephew.

---

* A History and Genealogy of the Habersham and other Southern Families, by
Joseph G. B. Bullock, M.D., 1901.

BAILEY FAMILY (Ba)

Ba-I. CAPT. JOSEPH BAILEY, came to Carolina in 1670, with the first fleet. After taking up lands he was sent within the first 3 wks. to negotiate with the Spaniards at present-day St. Augustine, and was never heard of again. He was a linguist.

Ba-II. RALPH BAILEY m. ELIZABETH SEABROOK.

Ba-III. RALPH BAILEY m. MARY SPLATT.

Ba-IV. CAPT. BENJAMIN BAILEY, of Edisto Is., b. Apr. 1780, d. May 4, 1830, m. Nov. 4, 1801, (1) SARAH EATON PATTERSON, dau. of Mary Jenkins who m. Sept. 13, 1781, John Patterson, b. Nov. 8, 1786, d. Feb. 16, 1819. He m. (2) MARY WASHINGTON TOWNSEND, dau. of John Townsend and Elizabeth Reynolds.

Issue by 1st wife: SARAH EATON PATTERSON.

Ba-1. Benjamin John, d. Nov. 2, 1813, age 6.

Ba-2. Mary Jenkins, d. Aug. 1817, age 5.

Ba-3, 4, 5, 6. Three infant sons and one infant dau., unnamed.

*Ba-7. Ann Eliza, only surviving child, b. 1818, d. at Stono, Mar. 31, 1850, bur. Presby. chyd., Edisto Island, m. ca. 1837 Benjamin Bailey, her 1st cou., son of Edward Bailey and second wife, Susan Jane Patterson, dau. of James Patterson and wife, Abigail Townsend. Known as "Stono Ben Bailey", Benjamin was b. ca. 1815, d. ca. 1893. He m. 2ndly, Emily Amanda Jenkins, wid. of Thomas O. Bailey, younger brother of this same Benjamin Bailey, or "Stono Ben."

Issue by second wife: MARY WASHINGTON TOWNSEND.

*Ba-8. Martha Sarah, b. 1821, m. William Charles Bailey.

Ba-9. Elizabeth Lavinia, b. bef. 1825, m. in 1841, Robert Boone Jenkins, son of Christopher and Catharine (Boone) Jenkins, d. after 1865, no issue.

Ba-10. Susan Providence, b. Aug. 8, 1826, d. Aug. 20, 1851, n. m.

Ba-11. Mary Olivia, b. Mar. 12, 1828, d. Mar. 22, 1869, m. James LaRoche.

Ba-12. Benjamin, m. Carrie Scott, and had (A) John Scott, b. Mar. 28, 1855, d. Mar. 18, 1924, m. Florence Olivia Seabrook, b. July 22, 1856, d. Nov. 8, 1898, before 1884.

Ba-7. "STONO BEN" BAILEY and first wife, ANN ELIZA (BAILEY) BAILEY.

Ba-13. Theodore A., b. and d. 1838.

Ba-14. Sarah Eaton Patterson, b. July 24, 1839, d. July 25, 1914, bur. St. James' Ep. Chyd., James Island, m. 1857, Thomas Hanscome Grimball, leaving many descendants.

*Ba-15. Malvina Washington, ("Washie"), b. 1841, m. her 1st cou. Henry Bailey, son of Henry F. Bailey and Martha Hardy Mikell, b. 1836, m. 1861.

Ba-16. Julia Eva, b. and d. 1844.

Ba-17. Henry Mortimer, b. 1846.

Ba-18. Julia Ella, b. July 14, 1848, d. Feb. 27, 1935, m. Henry Julian Bailey, son of William Charles Bailey, (son of Edward Bailey and Susan Jane Patterson) and Sarah Martha Bailey, neé Bailey, (dau. of Capt. Benjamin Bailey and second wife, Mary Washington Townsend).

Ba-19. Ann Eliza, b. Jan. 1850, d. May 30, 1851.

Issue by second wife, EMILY AMANDA JENKINS whom he married 1853.

Ba-20. Alfred (or Albert) Rivers.

Ba-21. Oliver Franklin.

Ba-22. Ephraim Mikell.

Ba-23. Arthur M.

Ba-24. Archibald Hamilton.

Ba-8. MARTHA SARAH BAILEY m. WILLIAM CHARLES BAILEY, before 1844, b. 1817, son of Edward and Susan Jane Patterson Bailey, and d. Dec. 14, 1888. Edward and Susan Jane Bailey were also parents of Thomas O. Bailey, 1818-1852, who m. Emily Amanda Jenkins as her first husband. She m. (2) Benjamin Bailey.

Ba-25. Clarence, b. Nov. 25, 1844, d. Jan. 31, 1881, m. Mary Baynard, bef. 1872, b. June 24, 1850, d. Feb. 17, 1938.

Ba-26. Benjamin Washington, b. 1847, d. 1860, bur. St. Johns Chyd.

Ba-27. Rosa S. L., b. 1851, d. 1920, m. Edings Whaley, b. 1842 to William James and Martha Mary Murray (Clark) Whaley. He d. 1913.

Ba-28. Elvira A., b. 1854, d. 1920, m. George Washington Hills, b. 1848 to George Washington and Adella Beckett Hills.

Ba-29. Susan Providence, 1855-1931, m. Arthur Murray Whaley, b. 1847 to William B. and Martha Mary (Hanahan) Whaley.

Ba-30. Ralph, b. 1858, d. 1918, m. Gertrude Whaley, b. to Ephraim Mikell and Abigail (Baynard) Whaley.

Ba-31. Edward D., 1865-1925, m. Louise Whaley, 1854-1926, dau. of Edward Charles and Abigail Mikell (Whaley) Whaley.

Ba-32. Anne E., 1852-1899, m. Joseph Jenkins Wilson.

Ba-33. Martha Mary, 1859-1947, m. Joseph Jenkins Wilson as his 2nd wife.

Ba-15. MALVINA WASHINGTON BAILEY m. HENRY BAILEY, grandson of Edward Bailey, (1786-1830) and first wife, thought to be a Jenkins. Martha Hardy Mikell, b. 1815, of James Island, dau. of John Calder Mikell (1781-1836), and wife, Margaret Ann Mc-Leod, was mother of Henry Bailey. Henry, member of Company I, 3rd, S. C. Cavalry, C.S.A., d. of yellow fever in Charleston, Oct. 18, 1864.

Ba-34. Dau. who d. as infant, bur. Magnolia Cemetery, Chas.

Ba-35. Herbert Lee, b. 1864, d. 1919, m. 1893 (1) Lieze Mitchell, dau. of James D. Mitchell, m. (2) Martha Elizabeth Carrère, dau. of Charles Edward Carrère, attorney of Charleston and one of the early intendants of Mt. Pleasant, and his wife, Martha Elizabeth Purse. Charles Carrère was the only son of Dr. Maynard Edward Carrère and his first wife, Mary Wilkinson Legaré, eldest dau. of Solomon Legaré, of John's Island, and wife, and 1st cou. Eliza Slann Wilkinson Legaré, dau. of Col. James Legaré and Mary Wilkinson.

Issue by first wife: (A) Herbert Lee, Jr., of Summerville, S. C., m. Elizabeth Waring. Issue. (B) Henry Washington, (C) Waring Mitchell, d. unm., (D) Lise, of Summerville, (E) Winfield, d. unm.

Issue by second wife: (F) Augustus Legaré, m. Marion Hills, of John's Is. and had (a) Augustus L., Jr. of Cincinnati, Ohio. (G) Martha Elizabeth, m. 1937, Edmund Allan Burns and had (a) Mary Barbara Burns, b. Jan. 12, 1941, m. Charles Barry Nobles of N. J., and had Anne Legaré Nobles, b. Sept. 5, 1962. Martha Elizabeth (Bailey) Burns kindly furnished information on the family of Capt. Benjamin Bailey and his first wife, Sarah Eaton Patterson.

NOTE: The Bailey family is treated differently from others as far as tracing descent. When a Bailey married a Bailey, it is traced from the female line, not from the male line, as in all other families.

CORNISH FAMILY (Co)

THE REV. JOHN HAMILTON CORNISH, son of Dr. Andrew Cornish and wife, Rhoda, was b. Mar. 6, 1815, graduated Washington College (now Trinity), Hartford, Conn. 1839, ordained deacon St. Phillips Church, Charleston, S. C., 1842. Served numerous churches in S. C. but was longest at St. Thaddeus Church, Aiken, 1846-1865. Mr. Cornish married MARTHA SARAH JENKINS, in Trinity Episcopal Church, Edisto Island, Jan. 22, 1843.

Co-1. Rhoda, b. 1843, d. 1899.

Co-2. Martha Elvina, b. Aug. 25, 1845, m. John Gerideau Wilkinson, of Edisto Island, S. C., Feb. 6, 1879 and had (A) John Cornish, b. 1880, m. Lily Clark of Columbia, S. C., (B) Francis Allston Wilkinson, b. 1882, m. Violet Westcoat of Edisto Island.

Co-3. Elizabeth LaRoche, b. July 25, 1847, d. March 1848.

Co-4. Mary Amory, b. Dec. 13, 1851, d. Jan. 14, 1889, m. States Lee Baynard, of Charleston, S. C. and had (A) John Wilkinson, b. Feb. 12, 1883, (B) Joseph Cornish, b. 1884, d. 1885, (C) Mary Amory, b. 1886, d. 1890 and (D) Dr. Ernest Cornish Baynard, b. Dec. 12, 1888, d. 1928, m. Emily Whaley of Charleston.

Co-5. John William, b. Apr. 4, 1853, d. July 21, 1872, while attending Porter Military Academy, of typhoid.

Co-6. The Rev. Joseph Jenkins, b. Dec. 9, 1855, m. Elizabeth Percy Hereford, Sept. 4, 1890 and had (A) Rowena Sterling, b. June 4, 1891, m. Arthur Budlong, (B) Joseph Jenkins, b. Dec. 1893.

Co-7. Sarah Mills, b. May 7, 1857, m. G. Washington S. Jenkins, June 10, 1885 and had (A) Sarah Marcelline Jenkins, b. Mar. 22, 1886 who m. Dr. George Cullen Battle.

*Co-8. The Rev. Andrew Ernest, b. Dec. 4, 1861, d. Oct. 1920, m. (1) Sept. 12, 1889, at Sewanee, Tenn., Sarah Catherine Fairbanks, b. Feb. 11, 1858, St. Augustine, Fla., d. Jan. 6, 1918.

Co-9. Katherine Theodosia, b. Jan. 28, 1864, d. Feb. 16, 1948.

Co-8. THE REV. ANDREW ERNEST CORNISH m. SARAH CATHERINE FAIRBANKS.

Co-10. Col. George Rainsford Fairbanks, b. July 8, 1890, m. Helen Whaley of Charleston, S. C. and had (A) George Rainsford Fairbanks, Jr., b. Jan. 27, 1922, m. Esther McDowell Connor, b. Charleston, May 27, 1922, on June 5, 1948. Esther (dau. of Parker Ewan Connor and Esther Marion Seabrook) and George, Jr. had

(a) George Fairbanks Cornish III, b. Charleston, June 3, 1956, and (b) Parker Connor Cornish, b. Dec. 28, 1957.

Co-11. Sarah Catherine, b. June 10, 1892, m. (1) Richard Tyler Crawford, b. June 28, 1897, d. May 31, 1928 and m. (2) Richard T. King, d. Feb. 3, 1948.

Co-12. Gertrude Drew, b. Dec. 27, 1894, Charleston, S. C., m. the Rev. Henry DeSaussure Bull, b. Nov. 9, 1885, of Stateburg and Charleston, S. C. He died Apr. 26, 1957. Mrs. Bull kindly furnished the information on this family. She lives Georgetown, S. C.

Co-13. Ernestine Faith, b. Dec. 9, 1897, m. Chalmers Swinton Murray, of Edisto Island, S. C.

ELLIS FAMILY (E)

ELIZABETH CAPERS (Rc-14), spinster, dau. of Thomas and Mary Sadler Capers, m. EDMUND ELLIS of Port Royal, S. C., b. Aug. 26, 1724 to EDMUND and ANN ELLIS. Edmund I was bur. Aug. 9, 1737; Ann, bur. Mar. 31, 1738.

MARGARET ELLIS, b. Oct. 10, 1727 to Edmund and Ann Ellis, m. Sept. 6, 1744, NATHANIEL ADAMS, wid.

Another son of Edmund I and Ann Ellis, JOHN, b. Mar. 29, 1729, m. Sept. 2, 1752, ELIZABETH REYNOLDS, spinster and had (A) John, b. Dec. 1, 1753, bur. St. Helena, Oct. 18, 1757, (B) Elizabeth, b. May 11, 1755, who m. (1) David Adams and (2) April 1784, Daniel John Greene, son of Nathaniel and Susanna Greene. Daniel John Greene m. (3) Sarah Capers, Jan. 29, 1786, Daniel J. m. (1) Ann and had a dau. (A) Susannah, b. 1770 who m. 1787 William John Grayson and (2) William Joyner. (B) Daniel John, Jr., b. 1776, (C) Nathaniel, b. 1777, (D) Mary Greene, b. 1768 who m. the Rev. Stephen C. Lewis (Lewes). Daniel John Greene and Elizabeth Ellis had a son John, b. Mar. 19, 1785, bur. Mar. 20, 1785. Daniel John and Sarah Capers had Charles Thompson Ellis, bp. Feb. 15, 1787 and Robert Ellis, b. Apr. 29, 1790.

Issue of EDMUND ELLIS and ELIZABETH CAPERS.

E-1. Ann, b. Aug. 28, 1752.
E-2. Edmund, b. July 26, 1753.
E-3. Mary, b. Jan. 15, 1755.
E-4. Elizabeth, b. Sept. 3, 1756.
E-5. John, b. Mar. 3, 1757.
E-6. Eleanor, b. Apr. 13, 1758.

JENKINS FAMILY (J)

J-I. JOHN JENKINS, SR., m. ———— and m. 2ndly, April 12, 1727, ELIZABETH CAPERS ADAMS, widow of DAVID ADAMS, SR. and dau. of RICHARD CAPERS I and MARY BARNETT.

By his first marriage JOHN JENKINS, SR. had:

J-1. Ann who m. David Adams, son of Elizabeth Capers Adams.

J-2. William, m. (1) ———— Clark and m. (2) Mary Townsend and (3) Sarah Sealey, wid.

J-3. John, Jr., m. Mary Adams, dau. of Elizabeth Capers Adams. She m. (2) William Mason of Charleston, before Feb. 7, 1759. No issue.

J-4. Joseph, b. ca. 1714, m. Phoebe Chaplin. Issue.

J-5. Christopher, b. ca. 1716, lived St. Helena, S. C. and may have married a daughter of William Adams.

Issue by marriage to ELIZABETH CAPERS ADAMS, wid.

J-6. Thomas, living in 1735. No further record.

J-7. Elizabeth m. (? Ralph Bailey) of Edisto Island.

*J-8. Richard, of Edisto Island, b. ca. 1730, will prov. 1772, m. (1) bef. Dec. 4, 1750, Abigail, dau. of Daniel and Abigail Townsend; m. (2) bef. 1755, Martha, dau. of Edward and Ann Rippon of Edisto Island. She may have m. (2) ———— Hanahan.

*J-9. Benjamin, of Edisto, Charleston and Wadmalaw Island, b. bef. 1735, d. ca. 1782, m. ca. 1757, Mary, dau. of Joshua Grimball, deceased in 1757.

J-10. Charles, b. bef. 1735. No record.

J-8. RICHARD JENKINS m. (1) ABIGAIL TOWNSEND and (2) MARTHA RIPPON.

Issue by first wife:

*J-11. Daniel of Edisto, d. ca. 1801 m. (1) Hepsibah Frampton and (2) on Feb. 2, 1781, Martha, dau. of Benjamin Seabrook.

Issue by second marriage:

*J-12. Micah, 1754-1831, m. (1) Mary Ficklin and (2) in 1785, Margaret Meggett.

*J-13. Benjamin, Sr., of Wadmalaw Island, d. 1826, m. 1784, Hannah Fripp, b. 1764, dau. of John and Elizabeth Fripp of St. Helena.

J-14. Richard. No further record.

*J-15. Joseph, 1761-1828, m. in 1785, Elizabeth Evans, 1765-1826.

J-16. Isaac. No further record.

J-17. Elizabeth, m. Nov., 1783, Paul Fripp, Jr. Issue.

J-18. Ann, m. Nov. 7, 1783, James Laroach of Wadmalaw Island. Issue.

J-19. Sarah. No further record.

J-9. BENJAMIN JENKINS, Esq., m. MARY GRIMBALL.

J-20. Sarah Grimball, m. (1) Archibald Whaley of Edisto Island, bef. 1781 and had 3 children. Archibald d. bef. 1791 and she m. (2) Dr. Alexander McGregor.

*J-21. Benjamin, d. intestate bef. 1820, m. Martha Reynolds.

*J-22. Samuel, d. intestate before 1822, m. Jane Reynolds.

J-23. Mary, m. John Paterson, Sept. 13, 1781.

J-11. DANIEL JENKINS m. (1) HEPSIBAH FRAMPTON and (2) MARTHA SEABROOK.

Issue by first wife:

J-24. Daniel, drowned March, 1804, with half-brothers, Richard and Thomas.

J-25. Hepzibah, m. Daniel Townsend before 1801. Issue.

Issue by second wife:

J-26. Benjamin Whitmarsh, m. Providence E. ———— and had (A) Martha Seabrook who m. William Townsend and (B) Hepzibah Townsend who m. Benjamin Reynolds.

J-27. Thomas, drowned, March, 1804.

J-28. Richard, drowned, March, 1804.

J-29. Amarinthia, m. in 1813, William Wilkinson.

J-30. Martha S., m. Richard Laroche.

J-31. Sarah, m. Ralph Bailey.

J-32. Joseph D., m. Emily Reynolds and had (A) William R., M.D., who m. Eliza Laroche Jenkins, wid. of Micah Joseph Jenkins. No issue. (B) Amanda who m. (1) Thomas Bailey and (2) Benjamin Bailey, (C) Melvin, d. y., (D) Thomas, C.S.A., (E) Melvin II, m. Susan Wilson and (F) Cornelia who m. John W. Jenkins.

J-33. Mary, d. 1784.

J-12. MICAH JENKINS, of "Hope" and "Walnut Hill," m. (1) MARY FICKLIN, who d. Dec. 1784 on Edisto Island; m. (2) May, 1785, MARGARET MEGGETT who predeceased him. Issue by first wife.

J-34. Richard, d. bef. 1830, m. Phoebe Waight Jenkins, dau. of John Jenkins, (son of Joseph Jenkins and wife, Phoebe Chaplin), and wife, Mary Fripp (dau. of John and Sarah Fripp). Issue: (A) Micah Joseph, 1810-1853, m. Eliza Laroche and had issue, (B) John William, m. Eliza Sams and had issue, (C) Richard Henry, of "Racket Hall" plantation and Rockville, S. C., b. June 12, 1812, m. Mary Amarinthia Sarah LaRoche, 1822-1888, died June, 1868. Known as "Major Dick," Richard attended Partridge Academy in Conn., class of 1829. Large slave owner of Wadmalaw Island. He had 13 children, one of whom, the 7th, William E. Jenkins, m. Julia Jenkins, a dau. of S. Hamilton Jenkins. (D) Mary Caroline, m. John F. Townsend, (E) Benjamin Roper, b. 1815, (F) Daniel Field, b. 1817, m. Frances Esther Furman and had issue.

J-35. Martha Perry, m. the Rev. Paul T. Gervais and had issue.

J-36. Barbara Calder, 1784-1855, m. Benjamin Dart Roper.

J-13. BENJAMIN JENKINS m. HANNAH FRIPP, Jan., 1784. He was ensign in Edisto Island, Colleton County, Regiment in 1775, d. 1826/7.

J-37. Ann, m. Col. Joseph Whaley.

J-38. Mary, m. Thomas Bailey.

J-39. Elizabeth, m. (1) ———— Hanscome and (2) Paul C. Grimball.

J-40. Martha, m. Micah Jenkins, son of Joseph, 1761-1828, and wife, Elizabeth Evans.

J-41. Richard, m. Martha, dau. of James and Ann Laroche, his first cousin. Issue: (A) Benjamin, C.S.A., m. Adelaide Chaplin, (B) Ann m. Daniel P. Jenkins, (C) Richard E., (D) The Rev. Paul Gervais, m. (1) Jane McNish, and (2) ———— Guignard and (3) ———— Weston, (E) Sarah, m. E. W. Laroche, (F) John L., m. Mary Hanahan.

J-15. JOSEPH JENKINS, m. in 1785, ELIZABETH EVANS, dau. of John Evans.

J-42. Richard, b. 1786.

*J-43. Senator and Col. Joseph, 1793-1874, m. Ann Jenkins Fripp, his first cousin, dau. of Paul Fripp and wife Elizabeth Jenkins.

J-44. Micah, b. 1796, of Mackay's Point plantation, married Mar. 27, 1817, Martha Jenkins, his cousin, (1797-1857), dau. of Benjamin Jenkins and wife, Hannah Fripp. Large slave owner. Issue: (A) Richard, (B) Ann, (C) Sarah who m. John Laroche, (D)

Elizabeth who m. Isaac Grimball, (E) Benjamin and (F) Micah, Jr.

J-45. Edward, M.D.

*J-46. John, 1794-1854, m. in 1824, Elizabeth Grimball Clark.

J-47. Sarah, m. John Laroche, her cousin.

J-48. Abigail, 1799-1897, m. George Mackay.

J-21. BENJAMIN JENKINS, b. before 1763, m. MARTHA REYNOLDS of St. Paul's Parish, Stono, who d. in 1842.

J-49. John T., of age in 1820, d. without issue bef. Dec., 1826.

J-50. William Rivers, 1818-1875, n. m.

*J-51. Benjamin James, b. ca. 1800, d. ca. 1847, m. Sarah T. Paterson.

J-52. Sarah Bailey, b. 1817, d. July 3, 1895, m. Nov. 1838, William Horace Rivers, 1817-1861, and had (A) William Horace, Jr., (B) Charles H., (C) John Douglas, m. Anne F. Jenkins, dau. of S. Hamilton Jenkins, (D) Susan, b. 1847, d. 1887, m. 1866, Dr. John P. Thomas, 1818-1900, as his second wife. They had (a) Lula, who m. in 1889, Claudius Bissell Jenkins, son of S. Hamilton Jenkins, (b) John T., (c) H. Rivers, (d) Farr, (e) Estell who m. T. T. Hyde, and (f) Martha Thomas, (E) Sarah P., (F) Lula, (G) Emily Rivers.

J-22. SAMUEL JENKINS, d. bef. 1822, m. JANE REYNOLDS (R-39).

J-53. Samuel, Jr., of Wadmalaw Island, d. bef. Dec. 4, 1818, intestate. He may have m. Dec. 3, 1817, Mrs. Lavinia Emma Whaley, of St. George's Parish.

J-54. Benjamin William, b. bef. 1801, m. 1836, Martha Ann Jaudon.

J-55. Daniel E.

J-56. Martha S., n. m., d. 1827.

J-57. William Seabrook, M.D., b. 1789, d. Aug. 15, 1814, m. (1) Martha M. Ogier, 1789-1811 and her sister 2ndly, Jane Keith Ogier, b. 1798. After Dr. Jenkins' death in 1814, she married John B. Ferrel. These were daughters of Louis Ogier, b. 1753, and his wife, Susanna Martin, 1764-1827.

William Seabrook Jenkins, M.D. and first wife, Martha M. Ogier, had a dau. Susan Martin Jenkins who m. George Thomas Anderson of Pendleton, S. C.

Robert Maxwell Anderson, son of George T. and Susan Martin Jenkins Anderson, was b. 1839, died 1890, m. in 1866, Emma Jane Holland, of Ninety Six, S. C. Their dau., Cornelia

Gillam Anderson, 1870-1945, m. in 1907, Clarke P. Cole and had a son, Clarke P. Cole II.

J-58. Elizabeth.

J-43. COLONEL JOSEPH JENKINS, 1793-1874, m. ANN JENKINS FRIPP.

J-59. William Evans, 1817-1841, m. Ann Ball Poyas. No issue.

J-60. Elizabeth Elvyre, m. Richard Laroche.

J-61. Martha Sarah, b. 1821, d. 1864, m. the Rev. John Cornish.

J-62. Joseph Edward, 1830-1894.

J-63. Paul Fripp, M.D., 1826-1878, m. Theodora Ash Burden King, 1852-1898, and had (A) Ada Augusta, m. Thomas Osborn Barnwell, M.D., (B) Joseph James, m. Olivia Swinton, (C) Paul Fripp, Jr., m. (1) Laura DeSaussure Bacot and (2) Gay Gilliam, (D) Hawkins King, m. Josephine Manigault of Charleston and had issue, (E) Elizabeth Laroche, d. y.

J-64. Edward Delegall C., 1828-1859, m. Martha Murray. Issue.

J-65. Micah John, b. 1829, m. Eliza Ann Bailey and had issue.

J-66. George Mackay, d. 1873, m. Louise Hughes. No issue.

J-46. JOHN JENKINS m. ELIZABETH GRIMBALL CLARK.

J-67. John, Major C.S.A., m. Marcelline Murray.

J-68. Elizabeth, m. E. D. C. Laroche.

J-69. Edward, M.D., d. 1904, m. (1) Isabella, dau. of Benjamin W. Jenkins, (2) Laura Wellsman and (3) Sarah Adger.

J-70. Abigail, m. Richard Laroche.

J-71. Micah, 1836-1864, Major-Gen., C.S.A., m. Caroline Jamison and had (A) Micah John, b. 1857, m. Natalie Whaley and had issue, (B) Robert D., b. 1858, m. Amarinthia Laroche, (C) W. E., b. 1860, m. E. Tobias, (D) Whitmarsh W., d. y. and (E) John Murray Jenkins, b. 1863, m. Clara Wade.

J-71A. Lydia m. Daniel LaRoche.

J-51. BENJAMIN JAMES JENKINS m. SARAH TOWNSEND PATERSON, dau. of James and Abigail (Townsend) Paterson, sister of Susan Jane who m. Edward Bailey of Edisto Island. These sisters were orphans and were brought up by their aunt, Mrs. Daniel Townsend, of Edisto.

J-72. Edward J., b. bef. 1826, d. after 1848.

J-73. William H., d. Nov. 18, 1857, Lecompton, Kansas.

J-74. Ephraim Mikell Bailey, b. Oct. 10, 1830, d. 1882, m. 1857, Mary Elizabeth Beckett and had (A) Alexander Hamilton, 1857 1900, (B) Julian Brailsford, 1865-1923, m. 1895, Susan Lining Dawson.

J-75. Edwin W., b. ca. 1826.

J-76. John Jenkins (Jenkins).

J-77. Elizabeth Adams, b. 1822.

J-78. Septimus Hamilton, 1829-1904, m. Mrs. Anne Manson (Gautier) Bailey, wid. of Charles Joseph Bailey, dau. of Peter Wm. Gautier, and had (A) Henry Bailey who m. Mary Eva Bailey and had issue, (B) Anne Floride who m. John Douglas Rivers, (C) Claudius Bissell who m. Lula Thomas and had issue (D) Julia, d. 1930, m. William Evans Jenkins, son of Richard Henry Jenkins and Amarinthia LaRoche, and had (a) William Hamilton, b. 1893, (b) Julian Gautier, b. 1895, (c) Annie Mason, b. 1898 and (d) Mary Amarinthia, b. 1907, (E) Susan, 1870-1956, m. Edmund Seabrook, dau. of Ephraim Clark Seabrook and Elizabeth M. (Seabrook) Seabrook.

REYNOLDS FAMILY (R)

There seems to have been at least two brothers of the Reynolds family in S. C. ca. 1704, RICHARD I and WILLIAM I. WILLIAM I m. bef. 1710, and had sons, (A) Benjamin and (B) William, Jr. Benjamin m. Mary—and had dau. (only child) (a) Jane, who m. William Reynolds, son of Richard Reynolds and Mary Capers (dau. of Richard and Mary Barnett Capers). RICHARD I, b. ca. 1672, came to St. Helena Island, S. C. bef. 1704, d. Apr. 16, 1758, married ca. 1702, MARY CAPERS. Issue:

R-1. John, 1702-ca. 1750.

*R-2. James, b. Apr. 18, 1704, d. Jan. 1739, m. (1) bef. 1730, Eleanor Stevens, dau. of Michael and Elizabeth Stevens, d. 1736; m. (2) Sarah Saxby.

R-3. Constantia, b. May 28, 1705, d. Nov. 2, 1741, m. ca. 1737, Francis Thomson (Thompson), English school teacher who d. after 1744. Constantia and Francis had a dau. Anne, b. 1737, who m. 1753, Charles Capers (Rc-11).

R-4. Alice, b. Sept. 10, 1706.

R-5. Sarah, b. Aug. 6, 1708, d. after 1753, m. bef. 1733, Sam Stevens.

R-6. Charles Capers, b. 1710, d. y.

R-7. Jane, b. 1711, d. y.

R-8. Benjamin, b. 1713, d. y.

*R-9. William, b. bef. 1722, d. Nov. 23, 1788, m. (1) May 8, 1744, Elizabeth Evans Trueheart, b. bef. 1726, d. in 1747.

R-10. Zacharias, b. 1723, d. y.

R-11. Philip, b. 1729, d. 1731.

R-2. JAMES REYNOLDS, m. (1) ELEANOR STEVENS and m. (2) ca. 1738, SARAH SAXBY who m. (2) April 1741 William Chaplin. By this last marriage James had a dau. Eleanor, b. 1738, m. Jan. 1756, Benjamin Chaplin.

Issue by first wife:

*R-12. Richard, b. Sept. 27, 1730, m. Sarah Thomas.

R-13. Elizabeth, b. Dec. 26, 1731, mar. Sept. 2, 1752, John Ellis, b. Mar. 29, 1729 to Edmund and Ann Ellis.

R-14. Mary, b. 1734, d. y.

R-15. Capers, b. Apr. 21, 1736, d. y.

R-9. WILLIAM REYNOLDS m. (1) May 1744, ELIZABETH EVANS TRUEHEART and (2) Aug. 11, 1748, JANE REYNOLDS, dau. of Benjamin and Mary, who d. after 1784.

Issue by first marriage:

R-16. Constantine, b. 1745, m. bef. 1784, Mr. ———— Scott.

*R-17. James, her twin, b. 1745, d. after 1784, m. Martha Oswald.

R-18. Jane, b. ca. 1746, d. y.

Issue by second marriage:

R-19. Elizabeth, b. Aug. 10, 1749, d. bef. 1784.

*R-20. Benjamin, b. Jan. 4, 1751, m. (1) Sarah Chaplin Smelie, wid. and (2) Ann Smelie.

R-21. Emma or Amy, b. Apr. 27, 1752, m. June 27, 1768, Paul Fripp.

R-22. Mary, b. May 11, 1754, d. y.

R-23. William, b. May 8, 1756, d. y.

R-24. Sarah, b. Apr. 10, 1758.

R-25. Jane, b. Nov. 14, 1759.

R-26. Martha, m. Apr. 24, 1783, John Boomer who d. in 1794.

R-27. Ann Mary, b. Apr. 2, 1764.

R-12. RICHARD REYNOLDS m. SARAH THOMAS, July 8, 1752, and d. ca. 1760.

R-28. James, b. Sept. 24, 1753.

R-29. Jonathan, b. Oct. 1, 1755, m. Hannah and had Richard who d. after 1798.

R-30. Richard, b. Feb. 11, 1758.

R-31. John, b. bef. 1766, d. Aug. 11, 1798, m. July 3, 1787, Mary Tray. No issue.

R-17. JAMES REYNOLDS, m. bef. 1770, MARTHA OSWALD, whose mother was a Tucker.

R-32. James, d. after 1784, m. Elizabeth Barnes.

R-33. Benjamin.

R-34. Elizabeth, b. Mar. 4, 1770, d. aft. 1804, m. John Townsend who was b. ca. 1764, son of Daniel and Susannah Winborn Townsend, and d. Dec. 22, 1824. They were married Feb. 13, 1787.

R-35. Martha, m. Benjamin Jenkins (J-21).

R-36. Sarah Providence, d. unm.

R-37. Mary, m. (1) Thomas Bell and (2) John Tailbird.

R-38. Richard, d. after 1784, m. (1) ———— and had (A) Sarah and (B) John, both of whom d. after 1861. He m. (2) Sarah

(Barnes) Oswald and had (C) Adeline E., who d. aft. 1897, m. bef. 1897, Judson Lawton, (D) Richard, d. Nov., 1861, (E) a dau. who m. Mr. ———— Peeples, (F) dau. who m. Mr. ———— Buckner.

R-39. Jane, b. bef. 1786, m. Samuel Jenkins.

R-20. BENJAMIN REYNOLDS, m. (1) May 3, 1774, SARAH CHAPLIN SMELIE, b. bef. 1759, dau. of William and Sarah (Saxby) Chaplin, wid. of Edward Smelie, d. Mar. 16, 1785. Benjamin d. June 28, 1826, bur. St. Johns Chyd., Johns Island. He m. (2) ANN SMELIE, dau. of William and Susannah Wilson Smelie who d. in Ala.

*R-40. William, b. 1776, m. Sarah Saxby Adams.

R-41. Harriet, m. Joseph Smelie Seabrook.

R-42. Eliza, d. y.

R-43. Thomas, d. after 1784.

Issue by second wife:

R-44. Mary Young, b. bef. 1792, d. after 1829, m. Mar. 21, 1807 Charles Gabriel Capers, Esq., who d. after 1829.

R-45. Elizabeth S., m. bef. 1814, George Alexander Chisholm Rivers, son of George and Ann (Evans) Rivers. She d. 1840.

R-46. Emily Ann, m. Joseph D. Jenkins.

R-47. Cornelia, m. bef. 1826, Benjamin F. Scott.

R-48. Martha, d. bef. 1824.

R-49. Benjamin, d. after 1820, m. in 1819, Mrs. Mary E. Chaplin.

R-40. WILLIAM REYNOLDS, m. SARAH SAXBY ADAMS in 1803, and d. in 1819. She was b. ca. 1785, dau. of Bernard and Elizabeth Chaplin Adams, and d. in Ala. after 1837.

R-50. Elizabeth Chaplin, b. Jan. 23, 1805, d. 1873, N. Y., m. (1) Apr. 19, 1821, Micah W. Jenkins and had no issue; m. (2) Mar. 5, 1829, John Trenholm Robertson who d. after 1837.

*R-51. Benjamin, b. Mar. 26, 1806, d. in Ala., Mar. 4, 1889, m. Jan. 19, 1832, Hepzibah Townsend Jenkins, dau. of Benjamin Whitmarsh and Providence E. Jenkins, d. in Ala., Sept. 25, 1887.

R-52. Sarah Adams, b. Jan. 6, 1809, d. Apr. 21, 1874, m. Dec. 1, 1825, William Sams.

R-53. Henrietta Catharine, b. Jan. 20, 1810, m. William Benjamin Townsend.

R-54. Bernard Adams, b. Feb. 11, 1811, d. unm. in Mobile, Ala., June 7, 1878.

R-55. William, b. Apr. 16, 1812, m. Mar. 12, 1840, Agnes Jane Peake, dau. of John Samuel Peake and Agnes Ewing, and d. Sept. 2, 1874. Issue: (A) John Peake, (B) Elizabeth m. Mr. ———— Wells, (C) Benjamin, (D) Hugh Alison, (E) Susan Townsend, m. Jenkins LaRoche, (F) Henry Peake, (G) William Townsend, b. May 9, 1858, in Ala., and d. in Charleston, S. C., Dec. 31, 1946, m. (1) Dec. 1, 1881, Elizabeth Jenkins Mathewes, b. Aiken, S. C., Nov. 28, 1859, dau. of John Raven Mathewes and Jeannie A. VanNess, who d. Nov. 16, 1949. They had (a) William T., Jr., (b) John Raven, (c) John Hertz, (d) Van Ness, (e) Lily, (f) Francis, (g) Jeannie Mathewes, (h) Archibald Seabrook, (i) Josephine Maybank Reynolds, who d. y.

R-56. States, b. July 11, 1814, d. 1850, Ala., in 1842, Anna Maria Peake.

R-57. Elivia Stititia, b. 1815, d. in La., m. Edward D. Bailey, b. after 1805, son of Edward and Susan Jane (Patterson) Bailey, d. in 1861, bur. St. John Chyd., Johns Island, S. C.

R-58. Julius Cornelius, b. Dec. 1817, m. Mary Elizabeth McCord.

R-59. Julia Emma, b. Sept. 27, 1818, m. Theodore B. Lee.

R-51. BENJAMIN REYNOLDS m. HEPZIBAH TOWNSEND JENKINS.

R-60. Benjamin, m. Sarah Alison.

R-61. Sarah Adams, d. y.

R-62. William Saxby.

R-63. Sarah Adams, b. Oct. 6, 1838.

R-64. Julia Ella, b. Oct. 18, 1840.

R-65. Elizabeth Chaplin, b. Feb. 6, 1843.

R-66. Rosalie, b. Oct. 28, 1845, m. Benjamin S. Herring.

SMITH FAMILY (Sm)

DANIEL LESESNE SMITH, M.D., 1877-1947, son of Samuel Porcher Smith, who m. Henrietta Ann Palmer, m. (1) April 14, 1904 ELIZA AMARINTHIA HANE, b. Oct. 14, 1874, d. Mar. 11, 1911, and m. (2) Sept. 12, 1912, MARGARET NETTIE HANE, her sister. They were daus. of Eliza Amarinthia Townsend of Edisto and Wadmalaw Island, S. C., and John Keitt Hane, of Ft. Motte, S. C. Margaret Nettie was b. Mar. 13, 1867, d. Nov. 10, 1951. Issue by first marriage only.

Sm-1. Daniel Lesesne, Jr., b. Sept. 20, 1905, m. Oct. 2, 1936, Clara Childs Ravenel, Sumter, S. C., b. Oct. 8, 1916, d. May, 1973. She was dau. of Theodore DuBose Ravenel, Jr. and Alice Childs, granddau. of Theodore DuBose Ravenel and first wife, Elizabeth Brisbane Fishburne. Issue: (A) Daniel Lesesne III, b. Jan. 14, 1938, m. Sept. 9, 1966, Ellen Virginia Hines, b. Jan. 24, 1940. (B) Alice Ravenel, b. Dec. 22, 1938, m. July 14, 1961, Dr. Frederick Gridley Phillips and had (a) Frederick G., Jr., b. Apr. 26, 1962 and (b) Robert Leland Phillips, b. May 1, 1965. (C) Clara Childs, b. Mar. 27, 1942, m. Feb. 20, 1965, Samuel Booker Carter, Jr., b. Aug. 2, 1934. (D) Theodore Ravenel Mazÿck Smith, b. Sept. 22, 1948.

Sm-2. Keitt Hane, M.D., m. July 31, 1932, Vivian Hoke, b. July 28, 1909. He was b. Nov. 14, 1906. Issue: (A) Keitt Hane, Jr., b. Feb. 19, 1936, (B) Vivian Hoke, b. Aug. 21, 1937, m. May 20, 1961, Daniel Rowls Luke, b. July 7, 1934, and had (a) Vivian Rowls, b. Aug. 22, 1963 and (b) Allison Keitt Luke, b. June 4, 1965. (C) Lesesne, b. Oct. 25, 1945, m. May 4, 1968, Saluda, N. C., Eugene McNulty Dickson, b. Nov. 20, 1941.

Sm-3. Samuel Porcher, b. Oct. 20, 1908, m. Oct. 24, 1931, Grace Emilie Howard, b. Dec. 23, 1912. Issue: (A) Emilie Howard, b. Mar. 17, 1941 (adopted), m. Roy Tedder, Sr., b. Aug. 23, 1938 and had (a) Roy Tedder, Jr., b. Nov. 30, 1958, (b) Angela, b. Apr. 8, 1962, (c) Daniel Ray, b. Sept. 26, 1965, and (d) Ruth Ann Tedder, b. Mar. 18, 1968. (B) Samuel Porcher, Jr., b. Apr. 26, 1942 (adopted), m. July 21, 1968, Peggy Jean Taylor, from Tabor City, N. C., b. May 4, 1946, and (C) Gordon Lesesne, b. Aug. 13, 1948 (adopted).

Sm-4. Nettie Hane, b. Oct. 24, 1910, m. Spartanburg, S. C., June 2, 1934, Marvin Alpheus Owings, Ph.D., b. Dec. 8, 1909, and had (A) Nettie Hane, b. Mar. 8, 1940, m. Aug. 13, 1960, George Stone Sweet, Jr., b. Nov. 26, 1937 and had (a) George Stone III, b.

July 21, 1964 and (b) Nettie Hane Sweet, ("Nanette"), b. May 16, 1968. (B) Amarinthia Lesesne, b. July 24, 1943, m. Mar. 2, 1963, Erik Francis Croen, b. Mar. 2, 1938, and had (a) Amarinthia Lesesne, b. Apr. 14, 1964 and (b) Erik Francis Croen, Jr., b. Dec. 18, 1966. (C) Marvin Alpheus Owings, Jr., b. Jan. 28, 1950. Nettie Smith Owings kindly furnished information on the Smith family.

This family is descended from RICHARD CAPERS and MARY BARNETT in the following manner.

1. Elizabeth Capers, m. (1) David Adams and (2) John Jenkins, Sr.

2. John Jenkins m. Abigail Townsend, dau. of Daniel Townsend, b. 1688.

3. Capt. Daniel Jenkins, m. Hepsibah Frampton.

4. Hepsibah Jenkins, m. Capt. Daniel Jenkins Townsend, b. 1751.

5. Dr. Daniel Jenkins Townsend, m. Susannah L. Swinton.*

6. Eliza Amarinthia Townsend, m. John Keitt Hane.

7. Amarinthia Townsend Hane, m. Dr. Daniel Lesesne Smith.

1. Elizabeth Capers, m. (1) David Adams and (2) John Jenkins, Sr.

2. Hannah Adams m. John Frampton.

3. John Frampton, Jr. m. Theodora Ashe.

4. Hepsibah Frampton, m. Capt. Daniel Jenkins.

5. Hepsibah Jenkins, m. Capt. Daniel Jenkins Townsend.

6. Dr. Daniel Jenkins Townsend, m. Susanna L. Swinton.

7. Eliza Amarinthia Townsend, m. John Keitt Hane.

8. Amarinthia Townsend Hane, m. Dr. Daniel Lesesne Smith.

NOTE: Susannah Lavinia Swinton, b. June 20, 1823, d. before 1867, was dau. of James Hunter Swinton, 1778-1825, who m. his cousin, 1804, Eliza Bailey, 1788-1845; granddau. of Hugh Swinton, 1737-1809, who m. in 1763, Susan Splatt, 1746-1822; and great-granddau. of William Swinton, the emigrant, and Mrs. Hannah Brown, neé White. William Swinton, b. in Scotland, was Kings Officer, Surveyor General of the Province and possessed a Barony of Land.

THOMAS FAMILY (Th)

JOHN PULASKI THOMAS, M.D., 1818-1900, m. in 1866, SUSAN RIVERS, dau. of Sarah Bailey Jenkins and William Horace Rivers, as his second wife. Issue:

Th-1. Sarah Farr, b. and d. 1869.

Th-2. Lula Evelyn, b. Dec. 1, 1871, m. in 1889, Claudius Bissell Jenkins, son of S. Hamilton Jenkins. Issue below.

Th-3. John Pulaski, Jr., b. 1872, m. 1906, Lottie R. Reaves.

Th-4. Horace Rivers, b. 1875.

Th-5. Sue Estelle, b. 1881, m. 1907, T. T. Hyde.

Th-6. David Farr, 1878-1889.

Th-7. Martha Reynolds, b. 1884.

Issue of LULA EVELYN THOMAS and CLAUDIUS BISSELL JENKINS:

(A) Claudius Bissell, Jr., b. Jan. 28, 1891, m. Nov. 10, 1914, Jeannie Black Hyde and had (a) Jean Hyde, b. Dec. 8, 1915, who m. William Melvin Martin who d. June, 1963, in Charleston, and had (1) Frances Jenkins Martin, b. July 29, 1937, m. Robert Hislop McDowell, and had Robert Hayden, b. 1960; Frances Jenkins, b. 1961; and William Neville McDowell, b. 1963.

(b) Lula Thomas, b. Sept. 4, 1918, m. Mar. 29, 1941, Charleston, Armin Franz Witte, Jr., son of Armin F. Witte and Hattie Sparkman. He was b. Mar. 23, 1918, Georgetown, S. C. Issue: (1) A. Franz III, b. Apr. 13, 1943, m. June 3, 1967, Cheryl Cooper and had Alice Naughton, b. May 11, 1970 and Anna Alexandria Witte, b. Feb. 24, 1972, both born Chicago. (2) Bissell Jenkins, b. May 13, 1946, m. Sept. 25, 1971, Linda Burton and (3) William Sparkman Witte, b. Oct. 27, 1949. All born Charleston, S. C.

(c) Minnie Black, b. Dec. 22, 1919, Charleston, m. Whitemarsh Seabrook Smith, Jr., son of W. Seabrook Smith and Gladys Tupper, and had (1) Jane Hyde, b. Nov. 10, 1948, (2) Whitemarsh Seabrook III, b. Feb. 17, 1944, m. Anne Frampton, Dec. 1970, (3) Sallie Huguenin, b. May 1, 1952, m. Joe Shisko, 1971 and (4) Ann Jenkins Smith, b. July 24, 1959. All born Charleston, S. C.

(d) Frances Hyde Jenkins, b. Feb. 10, 1927, Charleston, m. Daniel Tompkins Henderson and had (1) Frances Jenkins, b. Aug. 27, 1954, Charleston, (2) Daniel T., Jr., b. Feb. 5, 1958,

Columbia, S. C. and (3) Thomas Henderson, b. Jan. 2, 1968, Spartanburg, S. C.

(B) John Thomas, b. Aug. 4, 1892, d. ca. 1971, m. Nov. 5, 1913, Hess Waring Lebby and had (a) Hess Waring, b. July, 1914, (b) Lucille Lebby, b. June 30, 1929, and (c) John Thomas Jenkins, Jr., b. Sept. 2, 1928.

(C) Lula, b. Nov. 5, 1893, dec., n. m.

(D) Chilton Hamilton, b. Sept. 12, 1895, d. 1896.

(E) Charles Rees, b. Jan. 30, 1897, m. May 30, 1923, Elizabeth Noble Simons, and had (a) Charles Rees, Jr., b. Mar. 15, 1926 and (b) Arthur Simons Jenkins, M.D., b. Nov. 2, 1926.

(F) Lillie Eason, b. Oct. 7, 1898, m. Apr. 26, 1921, Edward G. Willoughby Middleton and had (a) Edward, Jr., b. Aug. 16, 1925, (b) Lill Jenkins, b. May 26, 19—, (c) Bissell Jenkins, b. Sept. 6, 1926 and (d) John Godrey Middleton, b. Mar. 31, 1931.

(G) Pierre Gautier, M.D., b. Nov. 4, 1900, m. Emmie Martin, dau. of Keitt O. Martin and Mae Carnes. She d. June, 1972, Charleston, S. C. Issue.

(H) Rivers Thomas Jenkins, b. Oct. 10, 1902, m. Feb. 21, 1925, Lewis L. Murchison, and had Lucia Murchison, b. Aug. 22, 1928 and Rivers Thomas, Jr., b. May 1, 1930.

TOWNSEND FAMILY (T)

ELIZABETH REYNOLDS, (R-34), dau. of James and Martha (Oswald) Reynolds, b. 1770, m. JOHN TOWNSEND, b. ca. 1764, on Feb. 13, 1787. He was the son of Daniel and Susannah (Winborn) Townsend, and d. Dec. 22, 1824. Their Issue:

T-1. Daniel, d. y.

T-2. Martha Seabrook, b. ca. 1789, d. Aug. 1840, m. (1) Morton W. Stobo, and (2) George Alexander Chisolm Rivers, b. bef. 1790, to George and Anna (Evans) Rivers.

T-3. Loirence Emma, m. (1) Archibald Whaley, son of William Archibald Whaley and Sarah Grimball Jenkins. Archibald d. without issue in 1808 and she m. (2) Dec. 3, 1817, Samuel Jenkins.

T-4. Susan Jane, m. May 20, 1828, John Samuel Peake, b. 1786.

T-5. Mary Washington, m. Benjamin Bailey.

T-6. John Richard Moncrieff, 1798-1832, m. (1) Mar. 9, 1820, Amelia Eliza Waring, dau. of Joseph B. and Mary (Ioor) Waring and had (A) Martha Cornelia. John Richard m. (2) in 1826, Mary Sealy (Seabrook) Clark, b. 1793, dau. of Joseph Baynard and Mary Joanna (Whaley) Seabrook, wid. of James Clark, and had (B) Joanna Adelida, b. Apr. 25, 1828, m. Oliver James Hart, M.D., son of Sarah G. S. (Clark) and William Rogers Hart, (C) infant, b. and d. in 1831.

T-7. William Benjamin, b. 1804, d. after 1886, in Ala., m. (1) Henrietta Catherine Reynolds, 1810-1833, dau. of William Reynolds and Sarah Saxby Adams and had (A) Henrietta Catherine Grimball, b. Oct. 14, 1833, d. after 1886, m. Mar. 11, 1852, Dr. Joseph D. Allison. William m. (2) March, 1835, Martha Seabrook Jenkins, dau. of Benjamin Whitmarsh and Providence E. Jenkins, and had (B) Harry, (C) William Benjamin, Jr., (D) Hugh and (E) Samuel Townsend.

T-8. Thomas, d. y.

T-9. Daniel, m. Mary Hanahan.

UNIDENTIFIED AS YET

Abstracts of Goodspeed's "Mississippi", 1891, lists:

LILLIE CAPERS, b. ca. 1873, of New Orleans, La., m. W. C. HAWKINS. Had lived in Ocean Springs, Miss.

LYDIA CAPERS, b. 1765, m. ELIAS DuBOSE.

WILLIAM W. CAPERS' will in Tuscaloosa Co., Ala. (Box for years 1821-1855).

CLAUD VIERS CAPERS m. FRANCES CAROLYN CAMP, Oct. 28, 1939, and had (A) Joseph Gerald, b. Apr. 17, 1947 and (b) Clare Dean, b. Dec. 29, 1949. From *A Family History*, John W. Boyd, 1968.

WILLIAM HENRY CAPERS m. ABIGAIL—and had
1. Charles William, bp. Jan. 29, 1798, St. Philip Parish Reg. (S. C.)
2. Priscilla Ann, St. Philip Parish Register.

GERALD MORTIMER CAPERS, PhD, author of *John C. Calhoun Opportunist: a Reappraisal*, 1960. Probably descendant of Thomas F. Capers who m. Amanda B. Mortimer, Nov. 12, 1828, by Mr. Dalcho.

JOHNIE CAPERS, resident of Ridgeland, S. C., b. Jasper Co., S. C., age 23 in 1918 (S. C. World War I Records).

J. HICKSON CAPERS, Major, 3rd Inf. Reg., C.S.A., 1861-1865, Arkansas.

AMELIA LeCUE whose former husband, WILLIAM CAPERS, deceased, is mentioned in will of George Mathewes, Charles Town, Gent., dated April 28, 1768, as 1 of 6 daus. of his sister Sarah Neale. Ann Jervey was a witness.

ELIZABETH CHARLOTTE CAPERS, wid. of the late CHARLES CAPERS, now residing in the City of Charleston when she wrote her will which was probated Aug. 9, 1858. Will also mentions Robert Austin, Trustee, and niece, Ann B. Cannon, wife of Theodore W. Cannon.

MARY E. CAPERS who married in 1828, WILLIAM JAMES. She was b. 1808, died 1838. Their dau., MARY PAULINE JAMES, b. Jan. 6, 1835, d. 1887, m., in Sumter, S. C., 1856, THE REV. JAMES McDOWELL, D.D., b. Georgetown, S. C., 1832, d. York, S. C., 1913. Mary Pauline James was adopted by Esther Louisa McCrea and husband, Dr. John Benoni Witherspoon. See *DuBose Genealogy,* MacDowell.

WILLIAM E. (JIM) CAPERS of Hendersonville, S. C., m. VIRGINIA WHILDEN and had a son who married and had ALEXANDER JAMES CAPERS. He married ELIZABETH PADGETT and had a son, ALEXANDER JAMES CAPERS, JR. who m. REBECCA NEELY.

JAMES CAPERS OF RICHMOND, VIRGINIA

Rt. Rev. Walter B. Capers writing in 1950, among other things, says that Bishop Ellison Capers and Bishop William T. Capers were six feet 1 in. tall, Henry D. Capers six feet and *cousin James Capers of Richmond, Va. was six feet two inches* . . .

DESCENDANTS OF GABRIEL CAPERS, THE FIRST

As indicated, one of the original brothers coming to America was Gabriel Capers, School Teacher. It also appears that he was married according to the "Prentiss" letter of 1899. His descendants apparently were few and unfortunately we could not include a record of them in this book. Perhaps some future clan member will revise this book and bringing it up to date can find more on Gabriel's line. This gentleman is not to be confused with the several Gabriels that appear in the lines of the original William and the original Richard which also include many Williams' and many Richards'.

DESCENDANTS OF COL. W. E. "JIM" CAPERS & VIRGINIA W. CAPERS

Also include according to advice received:

Miss Celestine Capers, Walterboro and Columbia College.

Miss Betty Capers, Walterboro and Charleston.

Although it appears that both of these ladies have married some years ago and have families we were unable to get their married names.

A MEMORANDUM

On The Life Of
WILLIAM CAPERS
Of The
AMERICAN REVOLUTION

William Capers (1758-1812) was the elder son of Richard Capers III and Martha Bordeaux Capers and of the fourth generation in America.

He was a descendant of the first William Capers who came from England to Carolina about 1679 with two brothers Richard and Gabriel. They were planters and school teachers.

The names appear in the Secretary of State's office in connection with grants of land and in the early records of the English Church in the Colony and the State. Subject's father and uncle being vestrymen in Christ Church Parish.

William Capers, the subject of this memorandum, was born in St. Thomas Parish, South Carolina, October 13, 1758 and appears to have lived there for some time as the records indicate he sold his plantation there about 1790 and moved to Georgetown where he engaged in rice planting for several years before moving to Sumter district where he devoted his efforts to cotton production. Affectionately known as "The Major" he died at his home "Woodlands on the Hills" near Stateburg on December 12, 1812 and is buried in the family (Capers and Guerry) cemetery. The grave has the seal or marker of a soldier of the Revolution. Several other graves there are also well marked.

This cemetery is located about eight miles north of the City of Sumter on the highway to Bishopville. The community is now (1965) sometimes referred to as "Staffords."

The following description of "The Major" is given in the Autobiography of his son, Bishop William Capers:

"A different kind of man was my father, whose name I cannot mention without emotion after 38 years since I saw him buried.

"I have studied his character with intense interest, and honor his memory in every feature of it with my whole soul.

"A chivalrous soldier of the Revolution was he, whose ardent patriotism cooled not to the last of life.

"And yet, after a few years in the Legislature following the establishment of peace, he held no civil office whatever and was seldom seen on public occasions, except in his office as Major of

Brigade, to muster the troops! He was a military man; the War of the Revolution had made him so, and to muster a brigade seemed his highest recreation. But no man I ever knew was more a man of peace than my father was.

"Social and unsefish, generous, and kind, his nature was impulsive, but it was the opposite of passionate.

"Benevolence supplied his strongest incentives, and the serving of others seemed to be his favorite mode of serving himself. I never knew him to be involved in a personal difficulty but once, and then it was on account of a wrong done by an unreasonable neighbor to one of his negroes.

"His education had been interrupted by the Revolutionary War and was therefore imperfect; but he had a clear and strong understanding, was fond of Natural Philosophy and Mechanics, wrote with ease and perspicuity, and in conversation was eminently engaging.

"He was born October 13, 1758, just the right time, he was fond of saying, that he might have a full share in the war of his country's independence.

"And . . . I am bound to claim for him that he fought with the bravest and best, first as a lieutenant in the Second Regiment when General Moultrie was Colonel; Marion, Lieutenant Colonel and Horry, a Captain and afterwards till the close of the War as one of General Marion's Captains and his intimate friend.

"He was one of the defenders of Charleston in the Battle of Fort Sullivan (Fort Moultrie); was in the Battle of Eutaw; was at the seige of Savannah, when Pulaski fell, and not far from him at the fatal moment, and was at the Battle of Rugely's Mills, which happened after his escape from imprisonment in Charleston, and before he had rejoined Marion.

"Indeed, he was there in search of Marion, whom he expected to find with General Gates, but found not as he had gone on an expedition to Fort Motte.

"At Stono, where the lamented Laurens fell, he was present and fought like himself; at Charleston he was one of its defenders and was one of those who accompanied Major Huger on the service; which, on their return proved fatal to that gallant officer, by a false alarm through inadvertence of a sentinel, whereby many lost their lives by the fire of their own countrymen from their own lines of defense besides numerous skirmishes which have never found a record in the books, though they contributed no mean quota of the defense of the country."

William Capers and his brother George Sinclair Capers entered the war for American independence very young. The records show they joined the cause at the beginning and served it well. The Daughters of the American Revolution have honored the former by naming a chapter for him.

REFERENCES

"*Saffell's Records of the Revolutionary War*, p. 293, etc. William Capers, First Lieutenant Seventh Company, Col. Francis Marion's South Carolina Regiment as it stood on November 1, 1779."

"*Saffell's Records of the Revolutionary War* is the highest possible authority on Revolutionary matters. Any direct descendant can become a Son or Daughter of the Revolution through this source." *(Ed. Note:* It is assumed if otherwise acceptable.)
"*Histman's Historical Register*"　　　"*Johnson's Traditions of the Revolution*"

CAPERS FAMILY—Francis LeGrand Capers (1908)—Pueblo, Colorado

Life of William Capers, D.D.—Wightman

Life of Marion—James

Marion's Order Book

The Soldier Bishop—Ellison Capers

CAPERS—GUERRY CEMETERY

Major William Capers (C-10), 1758-1812, was bur. Capers-Guerry Cemetery, Staffords, S. C. (near Sumter). His tombstone, a Daughters of the American Revolution marker, William Capers Chapter, reads:

Revolutionary Soldier

CAPTAIN WILLIAM CAPERS
1775-1783

MAJOR WILLIAM CAPERS
A patriot of the Revolution of 1776
Born in the Parish of St. Thomas
Oct. 13, 1758
Died in this neighborhood
Dec. 12, 1812

BISHOP WILLIAM CAPERS
of
SOUTH CAROLINA

BISHOP WILLIAM CAPERS (1790-1855) was the son of Major William Capers of the American Revolution and Mary Singeltary Capers.

Mary Singeltary Capers is buried near the Wando Community in South Carolina on the river of the same name.

Bishop William Capers left South Carolina College in his senior year when he decided to "read" law in the office of Judge John S. Richardson at Stateburg, South Carolina. At such time he was offered an army commission through General Thomas Sumter but refused when his father objected on the ground that the country was then not at war.

While a law student, young William Capers was invited to go on a "circuit" with a Methodist Circuit Rider and as a result ultimately became a minister himself. He had an active life. Among other things, he successfully established missions to the slaves and the Creek Indians. He traveled extensively the Indian territory, Arkansas and Texas. He became editor of the Southern Christian Advocate and was elected the official representative of the Church in America to the British Conference in London. W. M. Wightman, D.D., President of Wofford College, published an interesting book on the life of William Capers, D.D. and the era in which he lived.

Bishop William Capers was first married to Miss Anna White who died very young. Some time later he was married to Miss Susan Magill who survived him. They had five sons who were in Confederate service.

Bishop William Capers and his wife, Susan Magill Capers, are buried under the chancel of Washington Street Methodist Church, Columbia, South Carolina.

SUBJECT: Gen. Francis Withers Capers

REFERENCE: *History of Citadel*—Thomas

1892

This year, which near its close, that is on December 20th, was to mark the fiftieth year of the establishment of the Arsenal and the Citadel Academy, was destined in other respects, to be one of the most memorable in the history we are relating.

That which first arrested the attention of the officers and Cadets of the South Carolina Military Academy, beyond the routine of the School, was the death at a ripe age, crowned with honor and accompanied by troops of friends, of a former Superintendent, Gen. Francis Withers Capers, who in his Academic connection bore the more familiar title of "Major". On January 12th this distinguished soldier, scholar and teacher, and much beloved gentleman, ended his honorable and useful life—"died as he had lived, without ostentation and without fear, clinging trustfully to those he loved most, and looking humbly to the God and Saviour, in whom he most surely believed".

Born in the city of Savannah, Ga., on the 8th of August, 1819, Gen. Capers' record as elsewhere traced by the writer, shows how three States furnished the fields of his labors, and how five seminaries of learning became centres of his influence.

Our conception of his character as contained in the "In Memoriam to the Dead of 1891-92," is reproduced here:

His mind was quick in perception, broad in its scope, and tenacious in its grasp. He was a ready man. Hence mental alertness was one of his characteristics. He was an accomplished scholar. Possessing a fine imagination, with an element of poetry in his nature, he had the gift of graceful oratory in addition to that of sound speech. As a writer and lecturer, he was a master of good English. In him, as in Sir Philip Sidney, were combined the tastes both of soldier and student.

To brilliant mental qualities, General Capers added moral and religious traits of an elevated order. His sensibilities were keen and true, his sympathies deep and wide. He was a high, pure man. No one ever heard him utter an unworthy sentiment or knew him to act inconsistently with his fine sense of honor. His life was the illustration of "high thoughts seated in a heart of courtesy".

But the characteristic that invests his name with undying halo was that excellent gift deemed by high authority greater than faith or hope—the crowning grace of love. General Capers was a Christian man. His chivalry was Christian chivalry. Charitable in his judgments, he kept guard over his tongue and indulged in no wanton disparagement of his fellow man. Modest, unselfish, gentle and brave, he suggests a noble type of Christian manhood.

It was his Christian temper—his deep, religious feeling—that ennobled his life. And when old age came and reverses fell to his lot, it was Divine philosophy that gave him fortitude, that kept the Angel of patience hovering about him, and that finally glorified his death—making his own eve like "eve of Tropic sun".

A good soldier, a patriotic citizen, a true man, the fame of General Capers must rest chiefly upon his role as teacher—a role in its possibilities higher than that of warrior, or poet, or statesman. For forty-six years he engaged in teaching; to the instruction of youth in three States, but mostly in South Carolina, he dedicated his treasures of mind and heart. What better illustration of the influence he exerted than the grateful confession of one—himself an ornament of Church and State—the Rev. Ellison Capers, D.D., that of all men he owed most for the bent of his purposes and tone of his life to his brother, General Capers! Who then can measure the rich fruitage of his genius? In its fulness it must be unseen, unknown except to God. If he accumulated no money, he made men—high-minded men. If he was no builder of costly structures, he was a master builder of sun-crowned character. If he was denied in God's providence the prestige of public station, his was the heroism of a noiseless pursuit. The teacher's crown is his.

> "Like seed of laurel in the earth,
> The blossom of his fame is blown—"

But no need for him of stone or shaft. His monument stands immortal in the hearts and homes made better by his influence.

SUBJECT: Letter—Gen. F. W. Capers to younger brother Ellison
             Capers, Colonel 24th S. C. Vol.

REFERENCE: Soldier Bishop, page 87

COMMENT: Subject letter was written during campaign, prior to but
             leading up to the Battle of Atlanta (War Between The
             States)

NOTE: The boy "Odd" referred to in letter was the youngest brother
             who was killed at 2nd Manassas.
             The Bishop mentioned was Leonidas Pope, West Point
             graduate, who became Episcopal Bishop of La. He got a
             leave of absence and accepted a commission in the Confed-
             erate Army.

My Dear Ell:

Odd, so we call the dear boy who is gone, who sleeps at Manassas with
a surgeon's certificate in his pocket, that might have spared him to us;
remembering my bright, noble, beautiful captain, my gallant, true,
"aide-de-camp," the circumstances under which he wired me, and my
letter to ————; I cannot forgive ———— that he died. ————
should have made him his aide by all the memories of the Citadel. Oh,
how often in this life I have found it that my heart looked for responses.
None came. Thank God that blood is thicker than water. After waiting
with a note of Joe Brown's in my pocket for a boy from your General
Polk (who would have been glad to see me officially) waiting at
Resaca for General Johnston under the heaviest fire I could find, for
they had told me at his headquarters that the General had gone to the
firing, and that I would find him at or near Polky Hill. I went there and
found the heavy firing, but re-enforcements were coming up. By the
way, I never saw as much reason to admire your great bishop than I
did in the hour I passed there, and it proves what they say, that "blood
is thicker than water." Let me tell you the story as I have told it to
May. "Open your fire," said the General. He was addressing the captain
of a battery just above us on the crest of a hill, from the valley of which
our skirmishers had been driven in on the lines, and he was speaking
"fire" on the crest of the left opposite. "Our troops are climbing the
base of the hill; if I fire I open on them," said the captain. "Open your
fire," was the reply. By this time the hill opposite seemed to be on fire.
"Open your fire, sir," and the fire was opened. Stevens climbed the hill
by its aid, and while I was watching the climb and glorying in its
success, there came amid shot and shell the statement: "Walker's

[93]

division is crossing the river." I had been that morning under pretty sharp fire myself, but I forgot everything when I saw you. I went high on the hill to see, notwithstanding the "mosquitoes." Standing by that bridge upon your black horse, until all of your command were by, you sat as if upon parade. I did not think of Walker, the gallant fellow (who knew me). I saw him saluate splendidly. I heard the General say: "Follow the firing." It was then chiefly beyond us, but my soul was on that figure at the bridge. "Double quick your men," said General Polk; "this fire is very heavy." "Double quick your men." One of the handsomest sights I saw during the war was General W. H. T. Walker, saluting on the slope of that hill at Resaca. He was well mounted, always trim, and he took off his chapeau as if on parade. "Double quick your men!" was the first response. "Where shall I move?" asked General Walker, evidently supposing the order to "double quick" prospective. "Double quick your men, sir," was the only reply, and I have no doubt it saved many lives.

The most intensely *interesting sight* I saw during the war was that to which I have alluded, when you stood too long at that bridge, confound you, under the fire of, Sherman knows, how many guns.

(Signed) F. W. C.

NEW ECLECTIC MAGAZINE, MAY 1869

(Republished in S. C. Historical and Genealogical Magazine, 1902)
The Capers family of the South, and we believe it is exclusively a Southern family, made a remarkable fighting record during the late war. From the album of a friend we send you the following as embracing the members of this family who were soldiers under the red-crossed banner of Dixie, in the Confederate army:

2 Brigadier Generals
1 Colonel of Artillery
1 Lieutenant Colonel of Artillery
2 Colonels of Cavalry
1 Major of Artillery
1 Lieutenant Colonel of Cavalry
4 Captains of Cavalry
3 Captains of Infantry
3 Sergeants
2 Chaplains
3 Surgeons
14 Privates

Making a total of 37. These were without exception brothers, uncles or cousins. Nine were killed in battle, three died of wounds, two died of disease, thirteen were wounded more than once, seven were wounded once, and only three came through safe. Eleven of the officers were promoted for gallantry on the field of battle.

Life of Bishop William Capers gives an account of Captain William Capers in Revolutionary War.

BISHOP ELLISON CAPERS

ELLISON CAPERS descended from a family whose ancestors settled on the South Carolina Coast about 1690. He was born in Charleston in 1837, the son of the Reverend William and Susan Magill Capers. His school days were spent in Charleston and at Cokesbury. He graduated from the Citadel in 1857 and was appointed an assistant instructor. He married Miss Charlotte Palmer in 1859.

When South Carolina withdrew from the Union Ellison Capers went into the military. His service began with the firing on Ft. Sumter and ended four years later when Gen. Johnston surrendered in North Carolina. His military record includes battles fought at Secessionville and the S. C. Islands at the beginning of the war; in North Carolina, Georgia, Mississippi, Alabama and Tennessee with the Army of the West. The latter includes the battles of Shiloh, Chickamauga, Jonesboro, Jackson, Franklin and others. He had four years of active combat field duty, was wounded on three occasions and rose to the rank of Brigadier General, C.S.A. Most of the time he was attached to the 24th South Carolina Volunteer Infantry.

General Capers was elected Secretary of State in 1866 but resigned to study for the ministry. He was so ordained in the Protestant Episcopal Church and accepted a call to Christ Church, Greenville. The Rev. Mr. Capers' influence was not confined to his own denomination. After some years in Greenville and Selma, Alabama, he was called to Trinity Church in the State Capital. In 1888 he was made Doctor of Divinity by the University of S. C. and later became a member of the Board of Trustees. (*Hist. S. C. Military Academy* 1783-1892—Thomas)

According to Dr. W. P. DuBose in the *Sewanee Review:*

> "It is related that when he notified his old friend, Governor James L. Orr, of his determination to resign his office of Secretary of State in order to enter the ministry of the Church, the Governor's reply was: 'You will be a fool to do it. A man with your war record, personal magnetism and genial manners can command anything from the people they have to give. You can be Governor, Senator or anything you like. You will be a fool to give up all this to become a preacher.'"

(Quoted in the Book *"The Soldier Bishop"*)

In 1893 Ellison Capers was elected Assistant Bishop of South Carolina preliminary to assuming the position of Bishop. The press of the State voiced the sentiment of the people generally, in approving the choice of the Diocesean Convention in complimentary editorials including the following:

> "Bishop Capers is perhaps the most widely known and the most universally beloved man in South Carolina . . ."
>
> *Edgefield Chronicle*

> The consecretation of Bishop Capers at Trinity brought a vast audience of people from every quarter of the State. There . . . Methodists . . . Lutherans . . . Baptists . . . . Presbyterians . . . Catholics and Israelites present . . ."

Bishop Capers of South Carolina was elected Chancellor of the University of the South (Sewanee), a position of educational and ecclesiastical distinction, and while honorary, yet carried with it the opportunity for great influence. He was "a tower of strength" in the House of Bishops as indicated by tributes from other Bishops which are included in the book *"The Soldier Bishop."*

For example, from Boston, Mass., came this tribute from Bishop Wm. Lawrence:

> "Bishop Capers had a rather unique position in esteem of the bishops, certainly many of them. We Northern bishops, at all events, and I assume also the Southern bishops, looked upon him as a typical Southern gentleman of the best sort. He had done excellent service in the War . . . He was a man of wide experience. He had a right, therefore, to assume a position and authority superior to most men. On the contrary, he was one of the most modest, sensitive, self effacing men that I ever knew . . . one always felt his presence and his force of character."

Bishop Capers was often chosen to speak at commencements, Confederate reunions, battlefield dedications and the like. Many honors were bestowed upon him. His honorary degrees include the Citadel, The University of South Carolina, the University of the South at Sewanee. He was honored by Trusteeships and a U. D. C. Chapter at Florence was named for him. When he died in 1908, the tributes from laymen, press and the public were from all over the country.

In the *Columbia State* a beautiful tribute is entitled:

"CAPERS SLEEPS IN SACRED SOIL—
The South's great sorrow—The Reverend Head of the Diocese mourned by many of all creeds and stations in life."

and includes the following:

> ". . . It was an outpouring of love for the man who stood so high in the South as a soldier, a citizen and a churchman, combining all these qualities and with each winning honor and esteem . . ."

References: NOMINATION OF BISHOP CAPERS
S. C. History—(Sims)—(Wallace)
History of S. C. Military Academy—(Thomas)
The Soldier Bishop—Ellison Capers
Red Shirts Remembered—(Sheppard)
The Diocese—Bishop Capers Memorial—May 1908
History of the Protestant Episcopal Church in S. C.
The News & Courier Centennial 1962

ELLISON CAPERS
MAN OF GOD AND PRINCE OF THE CHURCH
1837 - 1908

Brigadier General C. S. A.
Secretary of the State of South Carolina
Priest of the Protestant Episcopal Church
Bishop of the Diocese of South Carolina
Chancellor of the University of the South
Trinity 1887 - 1893

The News and Courier
Charleston

1953

BACKWARD GLANCES
News our grandfathers read in
The News and Courier, Nov. 12, 1903

THE BISHOP'S PRAYER

An Editorial

"We humbly thank Thee, Almighty Father, for the past history of our country, and for the inspiring reflection that, notwithstanding the disappointments and sorrows of our Confederate history, we came through its great trial and struggle with our battered shields pure, our character untarnished, and nothing to regret in our faithful defense of the honor and rights of our Southland."

That was the prayer of Bishop Ellison Capers, former Brigadier-general in the Confederate Army, at the opening of the convention of the UDC yesterday morning. It is a prayer which every truehearted man and woman of the South might very well adopt in returning thanks and ascribing praise to the Majesty on high; a prayer which ought to be taught to the children of the South of this and later generations.

IN THE NAME OF GOD, AMEN!

I, Ellison Capers, of the City of Columbia, in the County of Richland, in the State of South Carolina, being of sound mind and memory and mindful of my duty, do hereby make, publish and ordain this, my Last Will and Testament, hereby revoking and annulling all previous wills and testaments and all codicils thereto, heretofore made by me—

Item 1. I give and devise my house and lot in the City of Columbia, where I now reside, to my beloved wife, Charlotte Rebecca, for and during the term of her natural life, and after her death to my executors and their successors in fee upon the following uses and trusts, that is to say: for the use and benefit of my daughter, Mary Videau Satterlee, for and during the term of her natural life and widowhood, and upon her death or remarriage, for the use and benefit of my grandsons, John and Charles Satterlee or the survivor, until the said Charles Satterlee or the survivor, reaches twenty-one years of age; then, upon the further trust to sell the said property and to divide the proceeds among my children who may at that time be living, share and share alike, the issue of any deceased child to take its parent's share, per stirpes and not per capita.

Item 2. The property in North Carolina, used by myself and family as a summer home, and known as "Camp Cottage", belongs to my wife and she will, after my death, make such use and disposition of it as she thinks best, but it is my expressed wish and desire that, so far as it is consistent with any use and disposition thereof that she may make, my executors will keep the said property as a summer home for the use of my children and their families, and that the said property shall not be sold except with the written consent of all my children who may, at the time of such sale, be living.

Item 3. I give and bequeath my Chicamauga sword and my crutches to my son, Frank F. Capers, to be disposed of by him in accordance with such written instructions as I have given to him or may heretofore give him.

Item 4. I give and bequeath my Episcopal ring to my son, the Rev. W. T. Capers.

Item 5. I give and bequeath the loving cup, given to me by the clergy of the Diocese of South Carolina to my daughter, Mary Videau Satterlee.

Item 6. I give and bequeath the silver set, given to me in Boston by Bishop Potter and his family, to my daughter, Lottie Johnson.

Item 7. I give and bequeath my watch and cross to my son, Ellison Capers.

Item 8. I give and bequeath my gold headed cane, presented to me by my friend, the late Captain Richard S. Desportes, to my son, Jno. G. Capers.

Item 9. I give and bequeath my small pocket silver communion set to my son, the Rev. Walter B. Capers.

Item 10. I give and bequeath the eastern candlesticks given to me by the late Rev. Churchill Satterlee to my son, Frank F. Capers.

Item 10-1/2. I give and bequeath my large silver communion set presented to me by the Sunday Schools of the Diocese of South Carolina, to the Sunday School of Christ Church, Greenville, S. C.—and I request that my Reverend Brother, Alexander R. Mitchell, present the same in my name, with expression of my hope that it will be a constant reminder that the Sunday School of Christ Church has trained some of our noblest communicants, and that I expect that this Sunday School will do as much in the future as it has done in the past in the work of the Master in that field of labor where the happiest days of my ministry were passed.

Item 11. I give and bequeath the pictures, "Christ on Calvary", "Christ before Pilate", "The Last Supper" and the Cathedral engravings to the Sunday School of Trinity Church, Columbia, with an expression of my love for Trinity Church and for the children of the Sunday School.

Item 12. I give and bequeath the portraits of my father and mother, now in the dining room of my home, and given to me by my sister, Susan, to my daughter, Mary Videau Satterlee.

Item 13. I give and bequeath the enlarged photograph of myself to my grandson, Ellison Capers Johnson.

Item 14. I have given the portrait of my father, which I purchased from Rev. M. T. Martin in Summerville, to the University of South Carolina, in which institution he was a professor in 1835, and I now confirm this gift.

Item 15. My wife has given the portrait of herself and myself painted shortly after our marriage to our son, Frank F. Capers, and I join in and confirm this gift.

Item 16. I give and bequeath all my books on theology and kindred subjects to my sons, W. T. Capers and W. B. Capers, to be equally divided between them. My remaining books, except my military library, I give to my daughters, Mary Videau Satterlee and Lottie Johnson to be equally divided between them.

Item 17. I give and bequeath my military pictures to the Ellison Capers Chapter of the Daughters of the Confederacy, Florence, S. C.

Item 18. I will and direct that the proceeds of my life insurance policy or policies and any currency or money on hand be applied to the payments of my debts and funeral expenses and to the payment of the mortgage upon my house and lot in the City of Columbia, and that the remainder, if any, be invested by my executors, the income to be expended for the use and benefit of my wife for and during the term of her natural life, and upon her death to be divided among such of my children as may then be living, share and share alike, the issue of any deceased child to take its parents share, per stirpes and not per capita.

Item 19. All the rest and remainder of my property, both real and personal, I give, devise and bequeath to my wife for and during the term of her natural life and upon her death to such of my children as may then be living, share and share alike, the issue of any child to take its parent's share, per stirpes and not per capita.

I hereby appoint my wife, Charlotte Rebecca Capers, and my eldest son, Frank Faysoux Capers, the executors of this will and give and grant unto them, and their successors, full power and authority to carry out the directions and provisions herein contained.

(Signed)

ELLISON CAPERS.

Signed, sealed, published and declared by
Ellison Capers, as for and to be his last Will and
Testament in our presence and in the presence of each
of us, and we, at his request and in his presence, and in the presence
of each other, have hereunto subscribed our names as witnesses
this the 16th day of December A. D. 1907.

Witnesses.

MARIE G. DWIGHT.

L. B. ZIMMERMAN.

J. WATIES THOMAS.

JOHN GENDRON CAPERS

Capers, John Gendron, United States commissioner of internal revenue, was born at Anderson, South Carolina, April 17, 1866. His father, the Right Reverend Ellison Capers, is the Protestant Episcopal bishop of South Carolina, who served as major, lieutenant-colonel, colonel, and brigadier-general in the Confederate States army, and was severely wounded in several engagements, was secretary of the state of South Carolina from 1867 to 1868, and entered the Protestant Episcopal ministry in 1867. His mother, Charlotte Rebecca (Palmer) Capers, was a collateral descendant of General Francis Marion. On his father's side he numbers Captain William Capers and Bishop William Capers of the Methodist Church, South, among his ancestors and kinsmen.

His boyhood was passed in the town of Greenville, South Carolina. Under the strong and loving influence of a mother whose touch upon his moral and spiritual life he has always felt, and a father who seemed to his son, as he expresses it, "a man of great wisdom and loving kindness in dealing with his fellowmen, of the highest integrity of character and of patriotism and courage, both moral and personal," the years of his boyhood were passed in study, with a great fondness from the first for history and particularly for biography; while a genuine boy's interest in the green things growing in the garden, and in the horses and the life of the place generally, at home, prevented studies from filling the whole horizon of his life, and early taught him to do some things with his own hands. He studied at Professor Mazyck's school, at Greenville; at Captain Patrick's military school, and at Doctor Porter's school (the Holy Communion Church institute), and the Citadel academy, in Charleston. He was graduated in law at Columbia, South Carolina, and was admitted to the bar before the supreme court in 1887. He was superintendent of education for Greenville county from 1887 to 1889. In 1893 he acted as editor of the Columbia "Daily Journal." For seven years, from 1894 to 1901, he was assistant United States attorney at Washington, District of Columbia, and in 1901 he was appointed United States district attorney for South Carolina, with his office at Charleston, in which office he served for one term.

When his successor as United States district attorney assumed the duties of that office, Mr. Capers' law office was at Greenville, South Carolina, and he in addition opened a law office in Washington, District of Columbia, devoting his time to the practice of law in both places.

He was engaged in the practice of law in this way, when, in June, 1907, President Roosevelt appointed him United States commissioner of internal revenue, upon the resignation of Honorable J. W. Yerkes, of Kentucky. Mr. Capers accepted the office for the short term, with the statement and understanding that he preferred the practice of law to government service, even in so high a position.

At first identified with the Democratic party, upon the nomination of Bryan in 1896 he became a supporter of McKinley and joined the Republican party. He shared in the campaign for McKinley and Roosevelt in 1900. He was delegate at large from South Carolina to the National Republican convention at Chicago in 1904, and he has been a member of the Republican national committee since 1904.

In 1889, Mr. Capers was married to Miss Sue Keels, sister of his brother Frank's wife, and daughter of John M. and Susan Maxwell Keels, of South Carolina. Always frail of health, she lived little more than a year. Six years after her death, Mr. Capers married Miss Lilla Trenholm, daughter of Frank H. and Mary E. Trenholm, of Charleston, South Carolina, and a granddaughter of George A. Trenholm, who was secretary of the Confederate States treasury in President Davis' cabinet.

There are no living children by the first marriage. By the second marriage there are two daughters, Charlotte Palmer, eleven years of age, and Frances Trenholm, eight years of age, at this time (1907).

Mr. Capers is a Master Mason, and a Knight of Pythias. He is a member of the college fraternity of Sigma Alpha Epsilon, and has been president of the fraternity and editor of its journal, "The Record." His church relations are with the Protestant Episcopal Church of America. He has found his exercise and relaxation, he says, "in the general out-of-door work about my little country home at Cedar Mountain, N. C.

—*Men of Mark in South Carolina*, Vol. 2
J. C. Hemphill (1908), pp. 62-63.

FROM: WHO'S WHO IN SOUTH CAROLINA

CAPERS, WILLIAM THEODOTUS, San Antonio, Texas, Bishop of the Episcopal Diocese of West Texas. Born Greenville, S. C., August 8, 1867, son of Ellison and Charlotte (Palmer) Capers. Educated: private schools; South Carolina College; Furman University; M. A., University of Kentucky; D.D. University of the South and Theological Seminary in Virginia, Alexandria, Va. Fraternities: Sigma Alpha Epsilon. President of the Province of the Southwest (ecclesiastical division); chairman of the committee from the House of Bishops on Placement of the Clergy; member of the Army & Navy Commission of the Protestant Episcopal Church. Member: Huguenot Society of South Carolina; American Historical Society, Inc. President of the Board of Trustees St. Philip's Junior College; president of the Board of Trustees of the Texas Military Institute; president of the Board of Trustees of St. Mary's Hall and member of a number of local institutions in San Antonio. Mason. Life member of Benevolent Order of Elks; Knights of Pythias. Sports: Horseback riding Clubs; Casino Club; Rotary. Author of Sermons and Addresses. Married Rebecca Holt Bryan, January 30, 1889. Children: George Bryan (deceased); Ellison Howe; Wm. Theodotus, Jr.; Samuel Orr. Home Address: 108 West French Place, San Antonio, Texas.

CAPERS, WALTER BRANHAM, Jackson, Miss., Clergyman. Born Greenville, S. C., Aug. 8, 1870, son of Ellison and Charlotte (Palmer) Capers. Educated: City School of Greenville; Furman University; South Carolina College; Virginia Theological Seminary; University of the South (Sewanee, Tenn.), D.D. In newspaper work 4 yrs.; deacon, 1897; priest, 1898, P. E. ch.; rector John's Memorial Ch., Farmville, Va., 1897-1901. St. Peter's Ch., Columbia, Tenn., 1901-11; pres. Columbia Inst. 1906-18; in charge Trinity Ch., New Orleans, 1918-19; rector St. Andrew's Ch., Jackson, Miss. since 1919. Deputy to Gen. Conv. P. E. Ch. from diocese of Tenn., 1907-10; same from diocese of Miss., 1922-28; same from diocese of Louisiana; trustee of All Saints College. Books written: "The Soldier-Bishop, Ellison Capers". Author of sermon, "Historic Addresses". Mason; Elk; Knights of Pythias. Episcopalian. Married Louise Drane Woldridge, June 29, 1904. Children: Hon. Walter Holdridge Capers, City Judge, Legislator, Sec.-Treas., Miss. State Bar Assn.; Charlotte Capers. Home Address: 705 N. State St., Jackson, Miss.

ELLISON CAPERS, JR.
(*The Second Ellison Capers*)
(1869 - 1918)

The following sketch is from the book *Men of the Time*, published 1902.

"Ellison Capers, Jr., was born in Greenville, South Carolina, May 9, 1869. Son of Bishop Capers. Attended the city graded schools, in Greenville, South Carolina; and from there, went to the Greenville Military Institute, then in charge of Captain John B. Patrick. While there he was so successful that, upon Captain's endorsement, he was chosen to assist Professor Cook, of Furman University, who had been employed by the D. Appleton Company to correct and verify the proof of Appleton's Arithmetic, then being gotten ready for the press. After a year's clerking, Mr. Capers entered Furman University, and took a high stand in his class. The following year he procured a school in the northern part of Greenville County, conducted it satisfactorily, and had made his arrangements to teach it another year, when his father received and accepted a call to Trinity Church, Columbia. Acting upon his father's advice, he gave up this school, and entered the University of South Carolina. He taught school in Clarendon County three years, after which he procured a position in the railroad shops in Columbia, where he worked for a considerable time. He then secured a school in Richland County, where he taught with great satisfaction. It was while thus employed that he became a candidate for county superintendent of education, and was elected over the former school commissioner, Mr. Sylvester. He was president of the Richland County Teachers Association. Before his term as county school commissioner expired, he was elected Principal of Winyah Graded School at Georgetown, South Carolina, which position he is now successfully filling. Married Carlotta Manigault Benbow, on June 9, 1892."

The second Ellison Capers (1869-1918) graduated at the University of South Carolina about 1890 and as indicated was school teacher, druggist, postmaster and had an insurance business.

It was not unusual during this time to find the Post Office located in the local Drug Store or an insurance business located in the Post Office.

These times were financially difficult in the South and this generation caught it hard, particularly those who made sacrifies to "scrape up" enough to insure that their children had a college education.

Ellison Capers (1869-1918) was a man who took sacrifices in his stride and thought little of them. He suffered from Brights Disease for many years but complained little. He was a man of strong character. He was blessed with a wonderful sense of humor and could be depended upon to find something amusing whenever possible to help brighten the day.

He would spot a shy person in a group and at once would make them feel better. He would dance with a "wallflower" and help the "underdog" in a sort of automatic thoughtfulness. He was a gentleman to the manner born.

A man of medium size, blonde with blue eyes, he inherited the good looks of his Mother. Always neatly dressed, he wore the derby hat, the high collar, the tie with stick pin, all appropriate to the times.

When it came to principle or justice or standing up for the right thing, he was a champion. He would for good cause, to use an old expression, "fight at the drop of a hat", and how important, how big or how powerful the adversary made not the slightest difference. He had too much courage for one man and he did not always win but usually dismissed any bitternes with good humor.

He had a keen mind and was delightful company. He enjoyed reading and was well informed. He found much happiness in "just plain living", adored his family and loved his friends.

After a long illness from influenza and complications he died at his home at Summerton, South Carolina, at age forty-nine.

ELLISON CAPERS III
(1893 - 1933)

On April 15, 1893, Ellison Capers, III, was born at "Valley Forge"—Clarendon County, South Carolina. His parents were Ellison Capers, Jr., and Carlotta Manigault (Benbow) Capers. It is so recorded in the family Bible in the clear handwriting of the Seventh Episcopal Bishop of South Carolina.

"Valley Forge" sounds like the humor of Ellison's father and was probably the name given a farm near Summerton operated as a side line to teaching school. This part of Clarendon County was the home of his mother's family and there were many lovable Aunts, Uncles and Cousins living there.

The older children in any family are usually lucky in that they get to know and remember their grandparents. Ellison was fortunate in coming along at a wonderful time for a boy. He received an illustrious as well as a euphonius name and was pointed out by one Grandfather as "this is my namesake" and the other as "this is my boy Ellison." As a little boy he rode in the saddle with his Grandfather Colonel William Washington Benbow and was therefore introduced to deer and fox hunting and the like at an early age. With plenty of available land, woods, streams, game and fish, Ellison, his cousins and friends, became avid hunters and fishermen. They trapped and captured many things. He brought home, according to his Mother, many wild creatures as well as a constant flow of dogs, goats, pigs, frogs and chickens, which kept his parents busy with the problems of reducing the managerie.

He received his education at Clemson College and the University of the South at Sewanee. He was not inclined to give priority to the studious side of college life, nor was it necessary as he had a very bright mind and he did not "have to" study like the less fortunate student. He made good marks but without neglect of social activities. He had a flair for adventure and joined the army in the short-lived "Mexican trouble" about 1916 and after a few months returned to civilian life and went to work. He began to settle down.

World War I found him again a volunteer and getting a waiver for underweight he was off again and right up from the ranks was commissioned First Lieutenant. He kept up his reserve commission promotions afterwards.

Subsequent to World War I he sold his insurance business in Columbia to become associated with the Board of Public Welfare succeeding to the top job of Secretary. During his career he had some good appointments such as Secretary, Board of Public Welfare, Superintendent, Columbia Hospital, State Hotel Inspector.

Ellison Capers, III, was a gentleman of sterling character. He enjoyed moving in the right circles and did so—and he like going first class—which he did. He was a "neat dresser", had a pleasing personality and was by nature of a frank and honest disposition. He was outgoing and thoughtful; he liked people and had a wide circle of loyal friends, many of whom were the outstanding and prominent of the State. He was known and liked by the great and the near great as well as a host of people in all walks of life.

Among other things, he was a member of the Kappa Alpha Fraternity, the American Legion and Reserve Association. He was a Mason and a Shriner as well.

Having learned early to enjoy hunting and fishing he was ready to go anytime and his years were filled with such happy events. He had a surprising amount of energy and out walked many a hunting companion. On June 2, 1920, Ellison Capers, III, and Miss Catherine Rice were married in Columbia and to this union two sons were born: Ellison, IV, who became a career officer in the United States Navy and Samuel Rice Capers, young businessman, who died at age thirty.

In the prime of life Ellison, III, was the victim of a traffic accident and died in the Columbia Hospital where he had been Superintendent. Ironically over the entrance of the hospital on Hampton Street is cut in stone "1893 Columbia Hospital 1933"—which were the years of his life.

THE STATE MAGAZINE
September 5, 1954

_____ A FATHER _____ A FAMILY _____

AND A FRESHMAN _____

By SAMUEL L. PRINCE
Dean of the Law School
University of South Carolina

Son to Father, "Where shall I go to school?" Father to Son, "The more important question: What will you do when you go to school?"

These are but extracts from a century old correspondence between William Capers, a bishop of the Methodist church, and his youngest son, Ellison, who later became a bishop of the Episcopal church.

There is a Chinese proverb to the effect that if you want to know people read their family letters. This correspondence between father and son is of interest not only because this family was and is worth knowing but the letter especially of the father to the son is the delivery without dross of a great intellect and great heart to one who in time developed an outstanding mind and an understanding heart.

William Capers entered South Carolina College (now University) in 1805 and left in his senior year to study law. Just before entering the practice he took a journey with a Methodist preacher which wound up with his becoming a Methodist minister. At the famous Baltimore Conference in 1844 the Methodist church was divided and William Capers became a bishop of the Southern branch.

Bishop William Capers lies buried in the Washington Street Methodist church graveyard at Columbia. There followed him a line of descendants with such vocations and positions as: six ministers, mostly Episcopalians, three bishops, a head master at The Citadel, a member of the faculty of this same school, a secretary of state for South Carolina, bank president, a commissioner of Internal Revenue for the United States, a postmaster, a business manager of Columbia hospital, president of the University of the South, head of the archives department of the State of Mississippi, numerous descendants and husbands of women descendants fighting with distinction in the Confederate army in the Civil war and in the United States fighting forces since the Civil war up to this very date and including many officers, four of whom rose to the rank of brigadier general. Two of the women descendants married ministers of the Gospel and one of these husbands became a bishop in his church.

While Bishop William Capers was holding an annual conference at Sumterville, in 1853, his youngest son, Ellison, wrote and asked him this question: "Where shall I go to school? This was the bishop's answer:

BISHOP WILLIAM

To His Son, ELLISON

"My dear Ellison:

I, too, was sorry enough that I could not meet with you with your mother and take a day or two at home before coming hither to Conference; but it is now past and being so only serves to add one little instance to the thousands which had gone before it, to show that we had always better be content with only so much pastime as may be consistent with duty than sacrifice the least mite of a positive obligation to pleasurable indulgences. As far as you are individually concerned, I do not know that I should have found more pleasure in seeing you at home than I have felt in getting the present letter from you; and I answer it in the midst of the business of a conference session that you may have some proof of my appreciation of it. Only don't write so fast, but take more pains with your penmanship till you have, by use, acquired a fixed hand.

You ask me where you shall go to school. My dear son, the more important question. 'What will you do when you go to school?' You say, and you put it in large letters, that you were never born to learn Latin and Greek. How do you know? I am sure you were as well born as any of my children, and I have no doubt born for as much. Your difficulty in learning Latin and Greek proceeds wholly from a want of attention. You have not fixed your mind attentively on this word or that, this rule or that (necessary to be known), to retain them fixedly in your mind, but it is the result of habit, and this habit you must correct, or you will neither learn Latin and Greek, nor anything else. You are capable, Ellison, of learning anything, without this simple impediment.

Discipline is indispensable to knowledge, and when you have acquired the power over yourself to stand still when you want to run, to be silent when you want to talk, to rise early when you choose to lie late in bed, you will have gotten on the way to fix your attention on any subject which may be presented to you for study. And in this way, as in most all others, the advantage will be found to increase with the line of progress. You will find a high satisfaction in the knowledge you gain, and scarcely less in finding out that you have only to try and keep on trying to accomplish just anything you please. You may become at the age of your brother Frank (and I say it with the grestest regard for his talents and learning) as able a scholar and as smart a man in every respect as he. Go where you may or to whom you may, it is not in school or teacher to do anything of any account for you without yourself.

And this is what you have to do for yourself: You must discipline yourself to do what you dislike, and to do it with attention, for the sake of the benefits to be derived from the unpleasant and irksome duty. You must learn to study by learning to deny yourself. Fix your hours (not too many, but a few in a day at first), and use today for what it shall produce tomorrow. I would feel confident of your making an able man and an honor to all about you, if you would but do this with respect to books and study. May god bless you, my son. Let Oddy read this letter. Much love and kisses to mother, sisters and all.

Your affectionate father,

W. Capers"

What a wonderful thing for a son to have a father capable of such clear insight to training and willing to take the time from arduous duties to sit down and write such a letter and that in long hand.

What a wonderful thing it would be to be a teacher of students coming to college with such judgment and advice ringing in their ears!

BISHOP ELLISON CAPERS
To His Son, ELLISON CAPERS, JR.

Trinity Rectory
Columbia, So. Ca.
June 17th, 1890

MR. ELLISON CAPERS, JR.

My Dear Son:

In parting with you this morning, at the close of your college career, I wish to assure you of a father's blessing upon your manly and earnest efforts to do your duty to the opportunities which you have enjoyed *here*, and under Dr. Manly at Furman.

Your Mother and I appreciate, my dear Son, that you have made a *persistent* and *faithful* fight against the discouragements which a long habit of indifference to books and study made inevitable, and we have watched your fight, my Son, with all our hearts, and prayed for you daily.

I am entirely satisfied with your course and I feel all of a father's pride and hope in you. You have done your *duty*, and the knowledge and sense of that great fact gives me, as it will you, the highest satisfaction and the greatest comfort.

And my dear Son, *go on* in *duty*, in *faith*, and *hope!* Hold *fast* your confidence in labor, and above all hold fast to your profession of *Christ*. Never let go your hold upon the Church, and the duties you owe to God. Kiss Mother and sisters for me, and give my dearest love to your brothers and our little Bryan. I want you to take a richly *deserved* rest in the mountains; and as a sense of *duty done* makes our sleep sweet and our recreation delightful. I feel, my dear Ell, that you will be refreshed by your vacation; and being 3000 feet above me in altitude you may rise beyond me, my Son, in every noble virtue and intellectual attainment, until you and I, and all we love, "Come in the unity of the faith, and of the knowledge of the Son of God, unto a perfect man, unto the measure of the stature of the fulness of Christ." I recommend this whole passage to you. Take it as my parting prayer for you. Ephesians IV, 13, 14, 15 and 29, 30, 31, 32.

Goodbye; and God *forever bless, keep* and *guide you.*

Your devoted Father

ELLISON CAPERS

ELLISON CAPERS (1869 - 1918)
(The Second E. C.)

To His Son ELLISON CAPERS III (1893 - 1933)

June 9, 1914

My dear Son:

I have come home from the office rather early today and my mind is filled with thoughts of love for my wife and children. I would be overwhelmed with the responsibilities that encompass me, were it not for a consciousness of the many and great blessings that I have enjoyed.

Today 22 years ago, I took my bride and what a chance she took! But many a rough and stormy sea she has ridden with me and yet today is more beautiful than ever. Although beset by the most ferocious and deadly germs I still survive!

All the events that have transpired in 22 years fill my thoughts—I will go down as pretty much of a failure but I know what obstacles I have had to meet them with. It is natural to feel discouraged after so much fighting and so much effort, and self restraint, but I solace myself in contemplating my wife's devotion, her wonderful preservation and the possibilities of my children. Armed now with 22 years experience, I may hope not to have to undergo many a trial that has hurt and hindered me in the past.

But the compensation of all these years is held in balance by my two splendid boys and my 2 beautiful girls. Mamma and I have weathered the storm, we have landed our little barque with its precious crew of four. Our oldest boy has just set sail on his own little life boat, in an unknown barque on an unknown sea. How anxious we are about him and how we will follow him as best we can, on his course through life, and we would so gladly give him the benefit of our experience, if he would make use of it. We have gladly given you our best. Your sources of ability—an attractive personality—a good mind, a fair education and a loving disposition—these splended qualities can be nullified by making bad habits such as making bills that you cannot pay—etc.

Take my advice and learn to make the distinction between false pride and true pride. Live within your wages if it requires you to give up every social function. I fully appreciate the importance of social standing, but social standing built of such material will not stand the test of time, will desert you and defeat your best efforts just when you need it most.

Debts paid with borrowed money is not progress. The only way to catch up when one gets behind is to do without. Make a sacrifice now in order that in later years you may be independent.

I wish so much you were here wih us today—to be my best man! Em and Kit could be bridesmaids and Rusty could read the service and make his Mama promise over again to OBEY!

Well, my dear son, if you would follow my thoughts today—a most youthful bride and her reckless young groom, boarding at a country school house, here they lived for two years, then a failure in crops made a failure in schools—I moved to Columbia, worked in the R. R. Shop for a year, taught school for a year and swam the stormy seas of politics in Columbia for four years. Then to Georgetown, whose people were most delightful and whose boys lead me a chase, more than once putting my shoulders to the floor! Then back to Summerton represented by 11 years of mixture of Druggist, Insurance business, Postmaster, etc. Sickness of wife, child and self, including two introductions to the hospital have painted pictures on my memory that are often with me and serve to draw us all closer to each other.

Take with me a toast to a bride of 22 years. The truest wife and best mother that ever was.

We are all well and send you our dear love.

Devotedly, your Father

ELLISON CAPERS

WHAT TO TALK —

TALK HAPPINESS   The world is sad enough without your woes. No path is wholly rough. Look for the places that are smooth and clear, and speak of *these* to rest the weary ear of Earth, so hurt by one continuous strain of human discontent and grief and pain.

TALK FAITH   The world is better off without your uttered ignorance and morbid doubt. If you have faith in God, in man, or self, say so—if not—push back upon the shelf of silence all your thoughts till faith shall come. No one will grieve because your lips are dumb.

TALK HEALTH   The dreary, never changing tale of fatal maladies is worn and stale. You cannot charm, nor interest, nor please by harping on that minor chord—disease. Say you are well, or all is well with you, and God shall hear your words and make them true.

Bishop Ellison Capers must have been pleased with the above. He made many copies in his own handwriting and sent same to his children.

ADDITIONAL INFORMATION

The following family information was received too late to be included in its regular place.

ADAMS FAMILY: A descendant of David Adams, 1682-ca. 1720, and wife, Elizabeth Capers, (dau. of Richard Capers I) MARIE ELIZABETH HARDEE, b. Savannah, Ga., m. CLIFFORD ALONZO KING, b. Roswell, Ga. Issue: (A) Clifford A., Jr., (B) John Hardee who m. Mary Florence Fox ca. 1890, in Texas, and had 2 daus., (C) William Habersham, (D) Barrington, (E) Charles, (F) Marie Hardee*, and (G) Noble Hardee King.

*MARIE HARDEE KING m. ERNEST MAYER CLAYTON, June 2, 1909, Denver, Col. She was b. Oct. 26, 1885, Dallas, Texas, d. Jan. 11, 1972; he was b. July 8, 1883, Beaver Falls, Pa., d. May 7, 1958, Douglas, Wyo. Issue: (a) John Clifford Clayton, b. Mar. 6, 1918, d. Oct. 28, 1942, lost at sea during W. W. II., (b) Virginia Clayton, b. Mar. 14, 1910, m. (1) Edward A. Reynolds, June 2, 1930. He d. Jan. 9, 1952 and she m. (2), Oct. 28, 1955, Donald Sherman Marmaduke, b. May 16, 1920, and had (1) Edward Reynolds, b. June 6, 1931, m. Barbara Conaway, b. June 22, 1937, and had Michael Edward, b. Sept. 20, 1959 and Randolph Clayton, b. Aug. 4, 1961. Virginia Marmaduke furnished the information on the Adams-Hardee-King family.

(c) Edith Clayton, b. Mar. 10, 1912, m. (1) James D. Morton, April, 1934, and (2) Vernon Howard Knisely, Jan. 4, 1954. Issue first marriage: (1) James D. Morton, Jr., b. Apr. 23, 1935, m. Kay Barricklow, b. Apr. 21, 1936, and had Kimberly Sue, b. Oct. 9, 1958; Jaye Dee, b. Apr. 20, 1960; and James D. III, b. Apr. 19, 1964. (2) Margaret Morton, b. Aug. 21, 1936, m. John Picchetti, and had Kary, b. June 19, 1966, and Eric Picchetti, b. May 29, 1969. (3) John E. Morton, b. July 17, 1939, m. Charla Petranovich, b. June 8, 1944, and had Amee, b. July 31, 1966; Jennifer, b. Oct. 7, 1968 and her twin, Jocelyn, b. 1968. (4) Sarah Morton, b. June 20, 1941, m. Myles Paul Monroe, b. May 19, 1944. Issue of second marriage (Edith and V. H. Knisely): Jil King Knisely, b. Sept. 14, 1956.

(d) Mary Clayton, b. Sept. 27, 1922, m. Feb. 18, 1949, Albert Aaron Clough, b. Dec. 10, 1914, and had Bert Hardee, b. 1949, and Thomas Frederick Clough, b. 1951.

JENKINS-THOMAS FAMILY

THE REV. CHARLES REES JENKINS, sometime missionary to Japan, b. Jan. 30, 1897, Charleston, S. C., m. 1923, Columbia, S. C., ELIZABETH NOBLE SIMONS, b. May 16, 1899, Charleston, dau. of Arthur St. Julian Simons and Caroline Walker Inglesby. Issue: (A) Charles Rees, Jr., b. Mar. 15, 1926, (Tokashima), Kobe, Japan, m. Apr. 10, 1954, Betty Jane Marshall, b. Apr. 2, 1925, from Stanton, Va., and had (a) Charles Rees III, b. Nov. 25, 1953, Columbia, S. C., (b) John Marshall, b. Dec. 24, 1955, Columbia, and (c) Betty Jane Jenkins, b. May 10, 1958, in Montgomery, Ala.

(B) Arthur Simons, M.D., b. Nov. 1, 1928, Kobe, Japan, m. May 23, 1959, Columbia, S. C., Frances Blanch Skelton, dau. of James Owen Skelton and Janie Ruth Betsill. She was b. Feb. 12, 1934, Greenville, S. C. Issue: (a) Arthur Simons, Jr., b. June 28, 1960, Charleston, (b) Charles Pierre, b. Feb. 25, 1964, Beaufort, S. C., (c) Wade Rees, b. Aug. 30, 1967, Beaufort and (d) John Skelton Jenkins, b. Dec. 22, 1969, Beaufort, S. C.

(C) Elizabeth Simons, b. July 13, 1933, Roanoke Rapids, N. C., m. Feb. 6, 1954, Fayetteville, N. C., Thomas Ashford DeVane, Jr., son of Thomas A. DeVane and Catherine Fitzsimons Dixon, b. Sept. 6, 1928, Fayetteville, N. C. Issue: (a) Thomas Ashford III, b. Feb. 10, 1956, Greenville, S. C., (b) Charles Jenkins, b. Apr. 3, 1959, Asheville, N. C., (c) Elizabeth Simons, b. Feb. 3, 1964, Charlotte, N. C. and (d) Catherine Dixon DeVane, b. May 13, 1969, Charlotte, S. C.

JOHN THOMAS JENKINS, b. 1892, d. May 2, 1970, Charleston, S. C., m. HESS WARING LEBBY, in Charleston, dau. of Robert Bee Lebby and Hess Waring Mikell. She was b. June 23, 1894, Charleston. Issue: (all born Charleston) (A) Hess Waring, b. July 24, 1914, m. Robert Latané Montague, June 21, 1942, and had (a) Constance Adams Montague, b. Nov. 1, 1948, Asheville, N. C., who m. James Gilbert Baldwin.

(B) Lucile Lebby, b. June 30, 1920, m. Dexter Cleveland Rumsey, Jr., Dec. 21, 1940 and had (a) Dexter Cleveland III, b. Apr. 15, 1942, Charleston, who m. Bonnie Marie Hoyle and had Caroline Mitchell Rumsey, b. June 22, 1965, San Diego, Cal., and Dexter Cleveland Rumsey IV, b. Feb. 1, 1973, Richmond, Va., (b) John Jenkins, b. Dec. 1, 1948, Washington, D. C., and (c) Robert Lebby Rumsey, b. Jan. 9, 1953, Charleston.

(C) John Thomas Jenkins, Jr., b. Aug. 2, 1928, m. Patricia Dotterer, Feb. 13, 1955, and had (a) Susan Lebby, b. Sept. 14, 1955, and (b) Patricia Dotterer Jenkins, b. Sept. 9, 1959. Both b. Charleston, S. C.

PIERRE GAUTIER JENKINS, M.D., b. Nov. 4, 1900, Charleston, S. C., m. Oct. 15, 1934, Florence, S. C. EMILY SINKLER MARTIN, dau. of Keitt O. Martin and Mae Carnes. She was b. Eutawville, S. C. Jan. 23, 1912, d. June 25, 1972, Charleston, S. C. Issue: (A) Emily Martin, b. June 29, 1936, Charleston, m. April 13, 1957, Thomas Banks Hindman, Jr., son of Thomas Banks Hindman and Bennie Cato. He was b. Sept. 15, 1934, Chester County, S. C. Issue: (a) Linda Emily, b. Jan. 15, 1958, Alexandria, Va., (b) Catharine Jenkins, b. Sept. 13, 1960, Aiken, S. C. and (c) Thomas Cato Hindman, b. May 22, 1962, Aiken.

(B) Martha Thomas, b. Feb. 16, 1938, m. (1) Joseph Cecil Kennedy, Jr. of Columbia, S. C., and had Joseph Cecil III, b. Sept. 18, 1958. She m. (2) May 12, 1963, Paul Waldmar Hund, Jr., from Charleston, and had Paul Waldmar III, b. Feb. 27, 1964, and Martha Priscilla Hund, b. 1965. All born in Charleston.

(C) Suzanne Gautier Jenkins, b. June 29, 1945, m. Dec. 15, 1959, Oliver Jack Burwell, Jr. of Spartanburg, S. C. and had (a) Heather Burwell, b. Apr. 15, 1971.

RIVERS THOMAS JENKINS, b. 1902, m. in Columbia, S. C., LEWIS LANDRUM MURCHISON, b. Jan. 2, 1903, Anderson, S. C., dau. of the Rev. Hugh R. Murchison, D.D., and Lucia Landrum. Issue: (A) Lucia Murchison, b. Aug. 22, 1928, Charleston, m. James Macdonald, M.D., in Charleston, May 23, 1953 and had (a) Lucia Jenkins, b. Greenville, S. C., Apr. 30, 1954, (b) Margaret Wilds, b. Greenville, Sept. 19, 1955, and (c) Elizabeth Murchison Macdonald, b. Joanna, S. C., Apr. 10, 1959.

(B) Rivers Thomas Jenkins, Jr., b. May 1, 1930, Charleston, m. May 15, 1954, in Charleston, Dorothy Cason Lemon, and had (a) Elizabeth Landrum, b. Oct. 14, 1957, (b) Margaret Sims, b. Nov. 24, 1959, and (c) Rivers Thomas Jenkins III, b. Dec. 18, 1962. All born in Charleston.

DUPRÉ-STEVENS-BERRY: HELEN CAPERS STEVENS (S-1) m. DR. DANIEL ALSTON DuPRÉ. One child was FAYSSOUX STEVENS DuPRÉ, b. Nov. 27, 1880, Charleston, S. C., d. June 8, 1939, Spartanburg, S. C., who m. Nov. 20, 1907, in Winnsboro, S. C., ELOISE WOODWARD ELLIOTT. She was b. Dec. 15, 1881, Wnnsboro, dau. of Thomas Ketchen Elliott and Carrie Aiken, and d. Mar. 14, 1972, Union, S. C.

Issue: (A) Carrie Aiken, b. Aug. 20, 1908, Winnsboro, who m. James Anderson Berry, b. Feb. 6, 1910, Union, S. C. to Dr. Robert Reid Berry and Sarah Jane Palmer, July 29, 1933, Spartanburg, S. C. They had: (a) James Anderson, b. Dec. 16, 1934, Union, S. C., (b) Robin Reid, b. July 11, 1937, Union, m. Sandra Gene McLees, on Oct. 5, 1968, in Atlanta, Ga., dau. of Malcolm Eugene McLees and Ruby Nell Wood. She was b. Dec. 16, 1942 in Anderson, S. C. They had Bonnie McLees, b. Nov. 6, 1969 in Atlanta and Kathryn Anderson Berry, b. July 23, 1973 in Atlanta. (c) Barbara Capers Elliott, b. Nov. 21, 1939, Augusta, Ga., m. J. Bon Filio de Leyva, (d) Peter DuPré Berry, b. July 25, 1943, Augusta, Ga. m. Harriett Katherine Cave, b. Dec. 10, 1942, in Columbia, S. C. to Edward Perry Cave and Catherine Hines. They had Daniel DuPré, b. Aug. 5, 1968 in Ft. Lewis, Wash., and David Elliott Berry, b. April 16, 1971, Atlanta, Ga.

Other issue of Eloise Elliott and Fayssoux S. DuPré: (B) Helen Stevens, b. Dec. 25, 1912, in Winnsboro and (C) Fayssoux Stevens DuPré, Jr., b. Jan. 12, 1924, in Spartanburg, S. C.

INDEX OF NAMES IN WILLIAM CAPERS LINE
AND RICHARD CAPERS LINE

[121]

Due 28 Days From Latest Date